How to Cure Your Memory Failures

Dozens of Proven Methods from Two World Experts

Douglas J. Herrmann and
Michael M. Gruneberg

BLANDFORD

First published in the United Kingdom in 1999 by Blandford

Text copyright © 1999 Douglas J. Herrmann & Michael M. Gruneberg

Design and layout copyright © Blandford 1999

The right of Douglas J. Herrmann & Michael M. Gruneberg to be identified as the authors of this work has been asserted by them under the provisions of the UK Copyright, Designs and Patents Act 1988.

Distributed in the United States by Sterling Publishing Co., Inc.
387 Park Avenue South, New York, NY 10016-8810

A Cataloguing-in-Publication Data entry for this title is available and may be obtained from the British Library.

ISBN 0-7137-2803-5

Cartoons by Bill Newton

Edited by Maggie O'Hanlon

Designed and typeset by Ben Cracknell Studios

Printed in Great Britain by The Bath Press, Bath

Linkword Method (p.89) © Linkword Programme: Interaktive plc

Memory Failure Interview (p.119) © Cognitive Associates, Clinton, New York

Blandford
Illustrated Division
The Orion Publishing Group
Wellington House
125 Strand
London WC2R 0BB

Contents

Acknowledgements

We thank Herb Weigartner for his helpful suggestions for this book and for sharing his views about memory failures. We also thank Jonathan Schooler and Steve Fiore for transforming our autobiographical method into questionnaire format and for collaborating on the memory failures of people in general and of memory experts. We also thank the people who contributed to the book. These include:

Jan Gruneberg, Vicky Gruneberg, Jannette McCool, John McCool, Jayne Nantel (née McKnight), Jean Natusch, Helga Noice, Tony Noice, Jonathan Schooler, Graham Wright, Margaret Wright, Phillip Gruneberg, Catherine Fritz, Judy Swez – and others who prefer to remain anonymous.

We would like also to thank our editor, Stuart Booth, whose advice on the content and structure of the book was of considerable value.

Douglas J. Herrmann
Michael M. Gruneberg

On-going Investigations

Our investigation of memory failures continues. If you have experienced a kind of memory failure which you think we have not covered, please send a description to either one of the authors via the publisher. Who knows, your account may appear in the next edition of *How to Cure Your Memory Failures*!

Preface

This book aims to show the reader the many different causes of memory failure and what can be done to prevent many of them from happening again. Of course, there is no cure-all for memory failures and our approach is to illustrate the causes of memory failure by using examples taken from our own experiences and those of other people.

At first sight this might seem odd. If memory experts cannot cure their own memory failures, how can they help anyone else? However, the fact is that, by studying the reasons for these memory failures, everyone can reduce the likelihood of them happening again. If we ourselves had not learned from our memory failures over the years, we believe that we would have had far more of them.

Some of the methods outlined in this book helped us to remember better in the first place. We also hope that, by showing that memory failures can happen to memory experts, readers will become more tolerant of themselves and others when memory failures do occur. After all, if memory failures can happen to memory experts, they can happen to anyone!

Introduction

Memory failures have been a problem for the human race since time began. People in Ancient Egypt, Greece, India and the Roman Empire found memory problems so annoying that they prayed to memory gods to help them. Just a century ago, people had the same, or practically the same, memory failures as we do today.

In 1898, a psychologist wrote in the *American Journal of Psychology* about a variety of memory failures that people had reported to him. He noted that:

> *A young lady went to telegraph for an umbrella left on a car; she had been holding it over her head for 30 minutes. A lady walked into a parlor with a $10 bill in one hand, a match in the other. She put the bill in the stove and saved the match. A man picked up a pebble and put it in his pocket, took out his watch and threw it into the ocean. A boy returned from the store three times to find out what his mother wanted. A college professor, expert in numbers, is frequently seen with one black and one tan shoe on. A man walked home and left his horse in the village all night. The same man went home from church and left his wife.*

While people today do not pray to memory gods, or leave their horses in town, we are still bugged by the same problem of memory failures. Memory failures are of two basic kinds:

- Failure to remember something we previously knew, such as the name of an old friend we haven't met for some time.

- Failure to remember to do something, such as turn up for a date or a dental appointment.

The big problem with memory failures is that, at best, they can cause embarrassment while, at worst, they can be fatal. A very sad example of a fatal memory failure involved a pilot and co-pilot who were arguing so much while taking off from Heathrow airport that they forgot to adjust the flaps of their aircraft, which crashed, killing everyone on board. In another tragic case, a mother placed a carry-cot containing her baby behind her car while she unlocked the car door. She then got into the car, forgetting that the baby was still on the ground. As she backed the car out of the parking space, it ran over the baby, who died. More commonly, but no less sad, there are many sick people who die because they either forget to take vital medicines or forget that they have already taken them and inadvertently take an overdose.

A New Approach to **Memory Failures**

This book takes the view that everyone's memory ability – yours and ours – is less than perfect. However, not all memory failures are the result of so-called 'deficiencies' of the memory system. We sometimes fail at memory tasks simply because of bad luck. However, by looking at those factors outside our control and making sure that we are aware of them, we can reduce the chances of bad luck causing memory failures. It has to be said, too, that in many situations we can take action to overcome memory failures if they do occur. The new approach that we have taken in the investigation of memory failures involves analyzing personal accounts of real-life memory failures.

Using *Personal Experiences*

Accounts of people's personal experiences have been used by psychologists to study emotions for many years. However, they have almost never been used to study memory. We decided to take this approach after realizing that our own accounts of personal memory failures revealed causes of our forgetting that psychology did not fully explain. We believe that a scientific analysis of memory failures provides one of the best ways of understanding how to avoid such failures.

By examining numerous examples of our own memory failures and those of others, we have developed procedures for identifying the ways in which memory fails. As a result, we have identified a pattern of situations that lead to memory failures, a pattern that is relevant to everyone. A knowledge of how memory fails can prepare us so that it fails less often.

Identifying the Causes of *Memory Failures*

In order to identify causes of memory failures individuals are asked to:

- Write a full account of a memory failure which they have experienced. This may have occurred recently or in the past.

- Describe the context of the memory failure, specifically where they were, what they were doing, whether others were present, the time of day, and how they felt physically and emotionally prior to, and during, the occasion of the memory failure. These questions were derived from what modern theories of memory have indicated may produce a memory failure.

- Note any other possible factors which they believe might be responsible for the failure.

At the end of the book you will find a questionnaire, based on this approach, which you can use to interview yourself about the causes of your own memory failures.

Each memory failure is unique. Failures may have elements in common, but every failure has something peculiar to itself. Each memory failure presented in this book stands alone and tells its own story. After reading these accounts, it is apparent that no one – not even memory experts – can avoid all memory failures.

About **This Book**

We have both spent more than 25 years investigating memory, although our careers have been largely separate, with one of us in the USA and the other in the UK. As a result of a common interest in memory in everyday life, we met at an international conference in Wales and discovered a mutual compassion for the agony that people experience when their memory fails.

We agreed that virtually all memory books emphasize how to make memorization easy, but these books appear to pay little or no attention to the failures of memory. It seemed to us that what was needed was a book about how memory failures take place and how to avoid such failures. Books that make memorization easier are certainly worthwhile but memory failures are almost always inconvenient and often embarrassing, as well as sometimes very difficult personally. This book is devoted to minimizing your memory failures.

Organization

The first part of this book consists of over 60 examples of memory failures, all selected from our records. They have been chosen because we believe that they illustrate facts about how memory operates, how it fails and how such failures can be prevented. Many of the failures discussed are our own (Douglas Herrmann [D.H.] and Michael Gruneberg [M.G.]), while others were supplied by people whom we have interviewed. We have included our own memory failures because we believe that, by so doing, we will convince many readers that their memory is no worse than that of memory experts – a realization that should be a great boost to their morale!

The memory failures are grouped according to the effect that they have on a person's life. (Some failures affect the forgetter, shaking confidence or causing inconvenience. Some failures affect others, causing them inconvenience or annoyance.) Each memory failure is described, together with the reported reason for the failure and, after each account, we suggest ways of reducing the chances of the same kind of failure happening again.

The individual accounts are like short stories and, although they have not been selected to be particularly funny, interesting or sad, they often make entertaining reading. Nevertheless, we are certain that many of them will make you laugh because of the ridiculous situations that memory failures put a person in. Some will make you feel sorry for how bad luck conspired against the person, leading to unhappy or embarrassing consequences. Others will make you feel sympathy for the person because the results of the failure are sad. No doubt you will recognize some stories as being similar to situations that you, or others whom you know, have experienced.

The second part of the book explains how memory failures come about, summarizes the various reasons given for memory failures, and provides an overall view of the causes of memory failures and the principle ways of preventing them. By the end of this, you should have developed a good understanding of why memory fails.

The third part outlines some useful memory-improvement methods and steps you can take to improve your memory performance in everyday life. For example, you will be shown life-style habits that strengthen memory. Again, because memory failures are often due simply to being too mentally fatigued to concentrate on a memory task, better memory skills are presented to help you avoid mental fatigue so that your memory will fail less often. There are also useful tips on maintaining physical condition, health and memory, emotional states and memory, and social skills and memory. You will also be given mental techniques that will help your memory function better, so that you can avoid future memory failures, e.g. you will learn how to remember names and faces, telephone numbers, the meanings of foreign words and the spellings of difficult words.

Finally, there is a questionnaire which will enable you to analyze your own memory failures. Of course, we hope that, after reading this book, you will have no further need to do this!

Benefits of *Reading This Book*

By reading the accounts of memory failures, you will become more aware of the many factors, external and internal, that cause memory to fail. Such awareness, in our view, will prepare you to recognize those situations that might lead you to fail in the future. Once you recognize these situations you will be able to avoid memory failures. As you gain more experience at avoiding memory failures, you will become more skilled at avoiding them. You and those close to you will notice that your memory has improved. As you notice this improvement, you may find yourself checking certain parts of this book to make the improvement permanent and to make your memory better still.

We strongly believe that the information given in this book on how to cure memory failures can truly be helpful and, because it is drawn from recent research, the approach is both fresh and original. We are certain that our own memory failures would undoubtedly be worse if we had not used our expertise at least occasionally. Nevertheless, as we explain, although you can take steps to avoid memory failures in most situations, and despite the claims of some memory experts who promise that you can have a perfect memory, there are some situations in which nothing much can be done!

Part I | Real-life Memory Failures

CHAPTER ONE
Stories of Memory Failures

Stories of **Memory Failures**

Embarrassing **Incidents**

Often one of the main consequences of memory failure is embarrassment: we end up looking foolish in front of others. If the person suffering a memory failure is a memory expert, this embarrassment is even more excruciating, as some of the following accounts show. However, as the rest of the book will remind you over and over again, knowing about memory can certainly help you to overcome memory failure in many situations. Nevertheless, it cannot protect you from bad luck, distractions caused by others, tiredness, pressures of other demands and the many other factors which can cause memory failures. The important thing is that all of us can learn from the memory failures that we and others experience.

1. **What Did I Call My** *Memory Book?*

Donna and I went out to dinner with Scott and Ellen Kraly when they were visiting Manchester, UK, in 1986. I had been hard at work writing my memory-improvement book, which I had been calling an *Encyclopedia*

of Memory but had just renamed *Memory Mechanisms*. Over dinner I told Scott and Ellen about this book and the high hopes that I had for it. Scott asked me a natural question: 'What are you going to call this book?' To my great embarrassment, I could not think of the title. An incredulous Scott and Ellen were nearly speechless at my memory failure – not remembering the name of my memory book! Minutes later the title came to my mind.

Reasons for Memory Failure

While it might seem surprising that a memory expert could forget the new title of his memory book, it is not *that* amazing. I forgot the title of the book because:

- It had been a long day and I was tired and not concentrating.
- The recent switch in title had not really taken hold, so I could remember the old title but not the new one. *D.H.*

 ### Solution

We chose this example to start with because it illustrates so well that even memory experts can be embarrassed by memory failures. The fact that they can happen to anyone should be a comfort to everyone! Tiredness is a well-established cause of memory failures and memory failures caused by tiredness are difficult to avoid. Possibly the best strategy to adopt in this kind of situation is to claim that a final decision has not yet been reached! If you cannot bring yourself to tell a white lie when you forget something, or someone, you should know, the best strategy is to stall in order to give your mind time to work. A good stalling tactic is to change the subject quickly by saying something like: 'I am so tired of that book, let's talk about you; how was your trip?' One of the authors prefers lying in this situation; the other prefers stalling!

2. Forgetting to *Secure the Car*

I was suffering from a really bad ear infection and went to see the doctor. As I drove back, I was in a great deal of pain. I parked the car and went into the house. I spoke to my sister briefly, before she interrupted to tell me that the car was rolling down the hill! I obviously had forgotten to put the handbrake on when I parked the car. I flew out of the door and, to my embarrassment, the window-cleaner (whom my mother had sacked 2 days before) had jumped in the car and put the handbrake on.

Reasons for Memory Failure

Pain can be a major cause of distraction and hence of memory failure. Never blame yourself, therefore, if you forget to do something because you are in severe pain. *Anon.*

Solution

Being aware that pain can affect memory is important. You can then try to ensure that, when you are in pain, you pay extra attention, if possible, to matters of importance, such as medicines and appointments. It is also important to make allowances for others who have a memory failure caused by pain. People who are in continuous pain, such as sufferers from arthritis, should be given special consideration. If you have serious pain, try to avoid memory situations that are dangerous, such as driving a car. Try to have someone drive you. If you have to drive, be extra careful to check everything you do, such as signalling and looking in the mirror, as well as the controls of your car.

3. Failing to Do Up *My Zip-fastener*

Having spent a somewhat miserable year working in Dundee, Scotland, I secured a 'dream' job in Swansea, some 400 miles (640 kilometres) away in Wales. My wife and I put our house on the market and bought a new house in Swansea. We bought an old van and loaded all we could into it, ready for the long trip down to Swansea. Just as we were about to leave, the two elderly ladies from next door invited us in for a cup of tea to see us safely off on our journey.

My wife and I were sitting opposite each other when she suddenly noticed my zip-fastener was undone. Although nothing of great significance was exposed, it caused extreme embarrassment to both of us, since I could do nothing but cover the problem with my tea cup and saucer. Unfortunately, because of our embarrassment, we could not contain our laughter, much as we tried, so that my tea spilled onto the saucer, causing yet more embarrassment. The embarrassment was confounded with shame that we could not bring ourselves to tell the ladies what the problem was and they must therefore have assumed we were laughing at them. It was a poor return for an act of kindness to us and we both look back at the whole incident with regret.

Reasons for Memory Failure

'We were rushing to get out of the house because it was getting late and we were anxious to get going.' Forgetting to zip-up is a common memory failure, at least for men. In retrospect, I should have apologized, stood up, turned my back and adjusted my clothes. At least the ladies would not have felt that we were laughing at them.

I should admit that the same thing happened again when I had started to write parts of the present book. Our secretary pointed out the problem just before I was due to meet prospective students. However, she knows what I am like and was not the least embarrassed! Again the cause of the memory failure was distraction: I was in a hurry to take my wife into town when I last went to the toilet. However, the distraction reason does not really explain why, under similar pressure, almost all men do remember, almost all of the time, to pull up their zip-fasteners!   *M.G.*

 ## Solution

Always make sure to check your clothing after you go to the toilet. Make it a habit to look down! You might be surprised at what you see. (This advice applies only to men!) If you know that you have forgotten to zip-up, walk behind something, such as a table or a car, and surreptitiously check whether your zip-fastener is closed with your index finger. If it is not, excuse yourself and zip-up.

Men sometimes do this by turning away from the person they are facing. We know of a case where a headmaster taking an assembly suddenly found his zip-fastener was undone. He turned around and adjusted his zip-fastener, only to discover that he had forgotten that the girl's choir was standing behind him!

It really is a good habit to make sure everything is in order whenever you leave the bedroom or the bathroom. All men are susceptible to this failure for the same reason that children lose their mittens. They are in too much of a hurry or are dreaming of something else.

4. Shotgun *Eggs*

My husband asked me to hold a dinner party for his co-workers and boss. I spent the afternoon working in the kitchen. I took out the coffee-maker, washed some broccoli, put some rolls aside, and put the egg-heater – for making an egg-dish starter – on a burner on the stove. Shortly before people came, I started the coffee-maker, put the broccoli on low, put the rolls in the oven to heat, and put eight eggs, each in their own place, in the egg-heater.

When the guests arrived, I joined my husband in greeting them. I became very involved in talking to each couple or person as they came in. All of a sudden, we heard a loud bang like a gunshot in the kitchen, then two more bangs, then three more, and yet two more. Stunned, at first we all looked at each other and then we ran into the kitchen to see a cluster of egg splashes on the kitchen ceiling. It was obvious to everyone that I had forgotten to check the eggs while they were cooking. The eggs on the ceiling were worth a laugh but it also was very embarrassing. I never made that mistake again.

Reasons for Memory Failure

In addition to the distractions caused by the guests arriving, another, unstated, cause of memory failure in this case was having too much to do. Obviously, I should have taken into account the need to have been in the kitchen to deal with the eggs, and I should have excused myself immediately after greeting the guests. It is very easy to be caught up in social interaction and forget other matters. *Anon.*

Solution

Whenever social distraction threatens, it is important to instruct yourself to calm down and mentally check all your on-going tasks as soon as it is socially possible to do so. If necessary, excuse yourself to go to the toilet. It is a good idea to keep a cooking-timer in the kitchen, which you can set to go off a couple of minutes after a visitor arrives. When the alarm goes, it will remind you to return to the kitchen and your visitors will not mind you leaving them.

5. Arriving Early *at the Airport*

My wife and I were due to go on holiday with my brother and sister-in-law to Paris, France. They were to fly from London; we had booked to fly from Cardiff. The travel arrangements were made between my wife and my brother, and the tickets duly arrived and were stored in a safe place.

On the morning of the appointed day, we duly took our tickets and passports out of their 'special' place. We had previously talked to my brother about how much we were looking forward to meeting them, that we would meet in the hotel, etc. We arrived at Cardiff airport, parked the car, then presented ourselves to the booking-clerk at the desk. As she studied our tickets, she became very puzzled. She then excused herself for some considerable time, before reappearing to tell us that we were a day early for our flight. We had no choice but to drive all the way home and repeat the process the next day. The drive home involved a degree of recrimination as to whose fault it was. My wife gallantly agreed to take the blame since she had arranged the booking!

Reasons for Memory Failure

Clearly, as with most memory failures, a number of things went wrong:

- My wife's over-confidence that she knew the correct day may have been supported by talking to me and my brother about the trip – we did not raise questions about the day of the trip.

- I did not remind her to check, since she is normally highly reliable, and I presumed she would not make such a mistake.

- I did not take the responsibility of checking myself but, since I was going on the trip, I had equal responsibility.

This kind of memory failure often gives rise to mutual recriminations. Fortunately the error was the right way: we only had to turn up the next

day. Time and again, however, as in this case, there is no simple 'fault' when a memory failure occurs. *M.G.*

Solution

In all situations where two people are involved it is very important to reach an agreement that there will be joint responsibility for checking that all procedures have been gone through: checking passports are in order, checking the dates on the tickets etc. Checking may not have worked in this case, since the date of travel is something you do not normally make a mistake about, and there is an over-confidence that you have it right. You should always check everything.

A good way of being sure that you remember to check everything at the right time is to make a timetable of what needs to be done when and who is going to do it. Such a timetable should include the time of departure on your ticket. You should check before you leave that everything has been done.

6. Remembering a *Wedding Anniversary*

I once worked as an entertainer on a cruise ship and used to interview members of the entertainment staff in front of a live audience. On one occasion, I was interviewing a comedian, who mentioned that he was married. He described how he met his wife and that they had a wedding anniversary coming up shortly. I was totally caught by surprise when the

comedian asked me: 'When is your anniversary?' Even though I tried, at that time I was unable to recall the date. Needless to say, all the female passengers felt very sorry for me.

Reasons for Memory Failure

I was so caught up in the interview, I could not reallocate my attention to retrieval of personal information. Over-absorption in an on-going event can prevent you from remembering other things (the absent-minded entertainer syndrome).   *T.N.*

Solution

Relax as much as you can. Anxiety is a common cause of memory blocks, as anyone who is taking exams or who has had stage fright can tell you. The more prepared you are, and the greater your confidence, the less will be your anxiety. Again, the more you concentrate on what you are doing, the less likely you are to be affected by anxiety.

7. Leaving My Shoes *at a Memory Conference*

In July 1988 I bought a new pair of shoes. They were beautiful, and costly for our budget at that time. In August I attended the Second International Conference on Practical Aspects of Memory in Swansea, Wales. I took my new shoes with me but, because I valued them so much, I also took a second, older pair of shoes to knock about in. I wore the new shoes only once, on the day I gave a lecture. Otherwise I placed these shoes carefully under my bed in the room where I was staying.

On the morning of the last day of the conference, I put my suitcase on the bed and packed my clothes and souvenirs. Then I met up with the people I was travelling with and made my way to the airport. About a day later, after getting home, my wife asked where my new shoes were. Then I remembered that I had left them under the bed. She said that I should write or call to get the shoes back. I refused because I thought it was useless and that some caretaker would have picked them up. She suggested that it was because I was too embarrassed to admit to my memory-expert colleagues that I had left behind an expensive pair of shoes at an International Conference on Practical Aspects of Memory!

Reasons for Memory Failure

- I put the shoes under the bed, something I never do at home and so I did not see them when I was packing the suitcase on top of the bed. I could only have seen the shoes if I had deliberately looked under the bed.

- I was anxious to leave and go home so I did not make a thorough check of the room before I left. *D.H.*

Solution

Forgetting to pack everything when you leave a hotel is a very common experience, as this example shows. Make a checklist of all the places you must look at before checking out of your room, such as the bathroom, bedside table, drawers, cupboards, wardrobe, under the bed – even in the bed (for nightwear and jewellery). Give yourself time to do this. On short trips, it also helps to use as few places in the room as possible.

Blows to Self-confidence

Sometimes memory failure shakes your confidence in your memory abilities. This can happen where the result of a memory failure is serious or where the mistake is so elementary that it sows the seeds of doubt about the reliability of any of your memory abilities. Of course, the fact is that we all, at some time or another, have our confidence shaken by our memory failures for simple and obvious things. It is simply not sensible to worry about them. This is particularly true as we get older, when many people start to worry about having Alzheimer's disease after one or two simple memory failures. It is, of course, true that as you get older, your memory is not as good as it was, but then neither is your ability to run for a bus! Some increase in memory failures as you get older does not mean that you cannot cope well socially or that there is a major health problem.

8. The Airport *Parking Mistake*

My son, Leon, and I went to Frankfurt, Germany, from Heathrow to attend the Frankfurt Book Fair. Although I parked the car in the main parking area, I did not park in the designated area, because I found an 'easy' parking space. After parking the car we collected our luggage, but I did not make a written note of where I had parked because I thought it was such an easy place to remember. (It should be said that, 2 weeks previously, I had parked the same car in that same car-park on another trip to Frankfurt.) We returned home the next night at 11.00 p.m., exhausted (the aircraft was 4 hours late), and took the courtesy bus to the car-park. The car was not where I thought I had parked it, and we could not find it anywhere.

We enlisted the help of one of the car-park staff, who toured around with a van, looking for our car. When I said how sorry I was for the inconvenience caused, he brushed aside my embarrassment, pointing out that he had already dealt with 17 such memory failures that day, although he was not impressed that I had not parked in the designated area. The search went on for a considerable time because, in the dark, I had no idea where I might have parked the car. I was also confused because I had left the car in the same car-park only recently. I raised the possibility that the car might have been stolen, but this was dismissed out of hand when I told him it was an 8-year-old Mazda! Eventually the car was found in an area that neither my son nor I recognized.

Reasons for Memory Failure

Clearly a number of factors were operating to cause this memory failure, which might well not have happened if any one of these factors had not 'gone wrong', for example:

- If I had made a written note of the car's position.
- If I had paid much more attention to where the car was parked.
- If I had not parked my car in the same car-park on a virtually identical trip 2 weeks earlier.
- If the flight had not been so late that we arrived tired and in darkness (removing possible visual cues).
- If my son had made a mental note.
- If we had parked the car where we were supposed to!

This example is a particularly good illustration of how memory failures are often multi-causal.

Of particular interest in this case is that I was over-confident of my ability to remember where I had parked my car, just as my wife displayed over-confidence in a previous example. But this over-confidence was not necessarily irrational. I had parked my car previously on countless occasions without a memory failure. In the past, the time between parking and trying to remember where I had parked was relatively short – less than 2 days – and we usually arrived back in daylight. It could be reasonably argued that it was not easy for me to predict, on the basis of previous experience, that a memory failure would occur. The situation, just as much as myself, was 'at fault' in this memory failure.   *M.G.*

Solution

Forgetting where your car is parked is a very common memory failure. M.G.'s failure to find his car in Heathrow car-park is fairly typical and, in fact, his failure was the seventeenth that day! Obviously it is a failure that can be easily avoided by making a note of where you have parked your car or by using an electronic sensing device.

Memory Hints | **Finding Your Car in the Car-park**

1. Try to park your car in the same position, each time you park, in a familiar place, such as the supermarket car-park. If this is not possible, make an extra mental note, e.g. look at where you have parked in relation to landmarks, such as the end of the supermarket frontage.

2. In strange parking places, such as those at airports, it is advisable to write down the section you have parked in and, in case you lose the piece of paper, to make a major effort to make a mental note. For example, if the section is D6 you can use the Digit Letter Memory System to remember (see p. 93).

3. Make life even easier by buying a tiny recorder for your keychain. As soon as you park your car say into the recorder where you have parked the car. Alternatively, buy a remote control. Press it as soon as you enter the car-park and it will make your car horn sound.

---

9. Forgetting to *Wear Any Underwear*

My boyfriend and I were looking for a new car. After inspecting the one we liked we went home to discuss its purchase. We were so excited about it all and talked about the journeys we were going to make in the near future. Before we knew, it was 2.20 in the morning.

About 2 hours later, we heard a commotion outside. When we looked, an ambulance, a police car and a doctor's car had pulled up outside the house next door. Later that morning, at about 5.30 a.m., the ambulance and police had still not moved away and we realized that something serious had happened to our neighbour. In fact, she had died.

By this time, we had been up for most of the night and we were just about to settle down again to try and get some sleep when relatives of the dead woman arrived and were wailing in their grief. Needless to say we did not get any sleep at all that night! To make matters worse, when we did get up, I checked the mail and, with trepidation, opened the envelope that I knew contained my long-awaited essay from the Open University. Bearing in mind that I had received a very good mark for my last essay (81 per cent), I was expecting a similar mark for this one but, to my horror, it was only 50 per cent. I was totally demoralized by this. I then went upstairs, got dressed and left for work.

I arrived at work as usual and, about 2 hours later, needed to visit the toilet. To my surprise and total embarrassment, I found I was not wearing any panties.

Reasons for Memory Failure

Clearly distractions, tiredness and emotional tension played a part:

- I was totally distracted by the excitement of buying a new car.
- I was tired from not having slept the previous night because of discussions about the new car, the death of my next-door neighbour and the resultant commotion.
- I was demoralized by my essay result.

Solution

Be aware that, if you are tired or upset, you are more than usually liable to forget. Therefore, checking more carefully than usual is likely to reduce the chances of memory failures – but forgetting your panties . . . !

If you are in this frame of mind, you should always check your possessions whenever you move from one place to another. A possession check involves forcing yourself to feel for things like your wallet, keys, money, etc. Also, patting your clothing may cue you to remember other clothing that you might be in danger of leaving behind, such as your coat.

10. Careless *Driving*

In the winter of 1980, I spent some time in Canada and decided to rent a car as soon as I arrived. I normally live in Wales, UK, where vehicles are driven on the left-hand side of the road. The difference between driving on the right and on the left normally presents me with no real problems, especially if other cars are on the road (as they provide visual cues about which side of the road to drive on). One day, however, I was almost killed by a bus when I forgot that you should not turn left into a side-road without checking the oncoming traffic. Fortunately, the bus-driver was alert and avoided an accident.

Reasons for Memory Failure

Lack of concentration, thinking about other things and going back to earlier, learned habits all contributed to this memory failure. Driving on a different side of the road from the one you are used to can be difficult. Normally there is no problem if there is traffic on the road, but problems arise when a driver has to remember to change habits, e.g. at a crossroads or a roundabout. Many Americans have accidents in the UK. Similarly, many accidents in France occur within 20 miles (30 kilometres) of the Channel and involve British tourists, who are presumably going back to long-established habits as a result of anxiety to catch the ferry to England. They therefore ignore cues on when it is safe to overtake, etc.   *M.G.*

Solution

This kind of memory failure is, of course, life threatening. The problem occurs when there are no other cars around, so there are no visual cues to keep you on the correct side of the road. They also often happen once you are getting used to driving on the 'wrong' side of the road, when your concentration may slip slightly.

It is important to avoid distraction as much as possible, e.g. your partner shouting out that you have missed the turn-off! It is better to take a wrong route than to crash the car because you forget, as a result of distraction, that you cannot turn left (or right) against the on-coming traffic. The golden rule is never to relax when driving in a foreign country. Obviously, it is wise to drive more slowly, so that, if you do make a mistake, there is more time to correct it. One tip is to put a clothes-peg on the speedometer or drape a scarf around the mirror. This will remind you that you are in a different situation from normal.

11. 'Mother?'

When I was 17 years old, I spent 2 months on holiday in Germany. We lived in Edinburgh at the time and I travelled home by train. In London, I caught the train for Edinburgh, some 400 miles (640 kilometres) away, and was walking along the corridor when I came across a woman who looked very much like my mother. I thought that my mother was in Edinburgh, as she rarely, if ever, visited London on her own. So the situation presented me with a considerable problem. I did not believe that the person was my mother; she just looked like my mother. If I said 'Hello Mother' and it was *not* my mother, this would have caused me serious embarrassment. If this person *was* my mother and I failed to acknowledge her, my mother would be hurt. Fortunately, before I could make a serious mistake, my mother said 'Hello Michael.'

Reasons for Memory Failure

It is very well established that a change in context can make a huge difference to memory. Learning something in one room and being tested in another room leads to poorer performance than if learning and

Sometimes it is important to remember a face, e.g. when you are a witness to a crime. There are three major things you can do:

1. Make judgements about the person: nice or nasty, clever or stupid, mean or generous, happy or sad, etc.

2. Note the major features of the face: big mouth, thick lips, thin face, high forehead, etc.

3. Bring the face back to memory from time to time. Repeatedly remembering the face is likely to refresh the memory of that face.

remembering are carried out in the same room. In the present situation, there was much conflict between context and perception, and I doubted that what I was seeing and remembering was the real thing. A change in context can interfere with our being able to remember people's names. In Edinburgh I would have immediately recognized my mother for who she was.

M.G.

Solution

In this particular situation the strategy of saying nothing was undoubtedly the best one. If you cannot place someone very familiar to you, *don't* admit it. Instead try to gather clues and keep talking in the hope that a clue will emerge – it usually does. Ask the person what they have been doing since you last met, what they are doing that day and so on. While talking, try to think of the place where you last met the person. (See p. 45 for an account of how to deal with a memory block.)

12. When Memory *Experts Meet*

Donna, Mandy and I had just moved into a flat in Manchester, UK. I left for my very first day of work in an eminent researcher's laboratory. Because it had been raining, I took my umbrella when Jim (a memory expert) and I went out for lunch. Jim brought his as well. We had a delightful lunch, discovering things in common and making plans for the memory research which we were to do in the next year. After lunch we left the dining room, by which time it had stopped raining.

We returned to the department and talked the afternoon away. The weather was pretty good for the next 2 days but it rained the day after. As we looked through the window at the rain outside, Jim and I both realized we had forgotten to collect our umbrellas 3 days before. We returned to the faculty dining room and inquired at the lost-and-found office about our umbrellas, but with no luck.

Reasons for Memory Failure

I forgot because:

- I had put the umbrella in a closet that was off the entrance.

- I was not in the habit of carrying an umbrella.

- I don't like having to carry umbrellas.

- I was busy getting to know Jim.

- I may have unconsciously expected Jim to remember his umbrella (after all he is English!) and thereby have a natural reminder to take my own umbrella – a reminder which he unfortunately did not provide.

This is another case of vanishing cues. The umbrella was stored out of sight in a closet. The weather change ensured that the other cue (rain) vanished. Had it been raining when we stepped outside, the memory failure would have been averted and we would have returned to get our umbrellas. Also a failure of mutual social reminding (because both parties had a memory failure) contributed to the memory failure.   *D.H.*

Solution

Vanishing cues are a 'nightmare' cause of memory failure. It can happen to anyone and if you don't realize the cue has vanished there is little that can be done. However, if you make a cue vanish, e.g. by putting a bag under a table, then make a mental note while you are doing this. Sometimes, as in the case above, where physical cues (rain) vanish, there is little that can be done!

13. Forgetting the *House Keys*

About a year ago my partner and I were invited to our friends' house for dinner. We were due to be picked up at 7.30 p.m. but, as usual, the taxi came 20 minutes early.

On the day of the invitation my partner and I went to do some clothes-shopping. On the way back from town we decided to do a bit of food-shopping and to buy drinks for the evening. In the car on the way home, my partner and I had a particularly nasty argument. The argument was on-going and was inclined to flare up over insignificant things. We had been going through this 'bad patch' for several months and it was very upsetting.

When we arrived home just after 6 p.m., our moods were worsened by the fact that we could not shower or bathe because the timer on the central heating was not working and the water was cold. While waiting for the water to heat up, we managed to dissipate the tense atmosphere somewhat and 'made up'. We got dressed to go out. After making what we thought were the usual checks around the house (checking that the heating was off, the back door was locked, the windows were closed, etc.), we left the house to go to our friends' for dinner.

When we arrived at our friends' house, I placed our house keys on the dining table and petted their dog. We had a lovely evening and at about 1.30 a.m. decided that it was time to leave. We were both tired after a long day's shopping and we were both pleasantly under the influence of alcohol, although not drunk. We did not stop to check who had the house keys before we left. When we got home, *I realized that I had left the keys on our friends' dining table.*

Another argument ensued and, to add fuel to the fire, the taxi that had dropped us off had already left. My partner insisted on going round the back of the house in order to break in. He climbed over our garden gate (approximately 6 feet/2 metres high), opened it to let me through and then proceeded to find a suitable brick to break the dining-room window! Out of curiosity and a nagging suspicion that I had not locked the back door before leaving, I tried the back door. To my surprise, followed by horror, I had left the back door unlocked, although, fortunately, nothing inside had been taken. Needless to say, we had another blazing argument and slept in separate rooms for the night!

Reasons for Memory Failure

We forgot about the keys because:

- We were both distracted by our problems and the arguments that had been triggered off throughout the day.

- We arrived home later than anticipated and found that the water-heater had not worked, which delayed our getting ready to go out and made us later still.

- We both assumed that the other had checked all the doors, windows, heating, etc. Our friends' dog had distracted me so I did not make a mental note of where I had put the house keys.

- It was late, we were both tired after the long day and we were both under the influence of alcohol when we left our friends' house, all of which were casual factors in my not remembering to pick up the house keys from the dining table.   *J.N.*

Solution

This incident illustrates the multi-causal nature of most memory failures. It also signposts steps which can be taken to reduce the chances of them happening. Over-indulgence in alcohol dulls the senses, leading to poorer judgement and lack of concentration, a recipe for memory failure. Domestic arguments disrupt social cueing, distracting you from reminding your partner about what needs to be checked. Being aware that these factors can increase the likelihood of memory failures should at least lead to increased checking if such situations arise in the future.

14. Forgetting to *Hit the Brakes*

When I took my driving test for the third time I was extremely nervous. I found the fact that the examiner made notes while I was driving extremely upsetting and I kept trying to see what he was writing.

After a while, he made me pull to the side of the road where he explained that he was going to ask me to do an emergency stop and that he would signal this by banging his notes on the front dashboard while I was driving. I was then to brake as hard as I could and bring the car to an emergency stop, as if a child had just run into the road.

I carried on driving for some time, when, all of a sudden, the examiner banged on the dashboard. I continued driving for some time before realizing what he had done. I then asked him if he would mind doing it again, but he refused. I failed my driving test for, among other things, failing to do an emergency stop (and for forgetting the meaning of a bang on the dashboard).

Reasons for Memory Failure

I attribute this failure to:

- My very high level of stress.
- The fact that I was concentrating on driving the car so as to avoid trees, people, lamp-posts, etc. Because I was relatively unskilled at driving and the task, I simply forgot what the bang on the dashboard signified until it was too late.   *M.G.*

Solution

High levels of stress narrow the range of cues which you can process, leading to memory failures. Use calming strategies, such as taking deep breaths and imagining calm, pleasant scenery. Of course you should not do this on a driving test if it involves closing your eyes!

Annoying or Inconveniencing Yourself

A number of memory failures harm only the person having the failure. However, this can be at best inconvenient, at worst extremely annoying and frustrating, especially if there is no one to blame but yourself!

Forgetting things which come back to 'bug' us is something we all experience. You just have to be philosophical about them when they happen, accepting them as part of life's rich tapestry, and try where possible to ensure that they do not happen again (see Part III).

15. Forgetting *Footballers' Bathtime*

I once arranged for an attractive female student to conduct a study of the ability of professional football (soccer) players to remember football results. Previous research had shown that the more people knew about a topic, the more new information on that topic they would remember. We thought that professional footballers would have the highest degree of knowledge of football.

The local professional football club, Swansea City, agreed that, after a reserve match, which finished at 4.40 p.m., my student could enter the dressing room and have 20 minutes to explain what the football questionnaire was about before getting the players to fill it in. At 5.00 p.m. the players could then listen to the day's football results on the radio before being asked to recall as many scores as they could remember.

Although I used to play football regularly, I had completely forgotten that, immediately after a match, footballers strip off and have a bath. Although the football team was happy for the student to enter the dressing room while they were in the bath, and the student was also happy about the situation, the Swansea City officials were not! Probably they were worried about newspaper headlines such as: 'They could not score on the field, but, boy, you ought to have seen them try to score in the bath'!

Reasons for Memory Failure

This was due to my failure to recall what happened after a football match and therefore to anticipate the problems it would cause.   *M.G.*

Solution

It is difficult to see what could have been done to avoid this situation, other than realizing that, in any situation, it is important to remember every detail and to anticipate what problems might arise. However, in this situation, it is difficult to conclude that I could have anticipated the problem and acted differently. It is another case of hindsight being better than foresight.

16. Forgetting a *Dinner Engagement*

I forgot a dinner engagement at a friend's house and on the evening concerned my wife and I ate a full meal. Moments later, my friend phoned me to see where we were. I apologized for being late and we went to my friend's place, where we both had to eat another meal!

Reasons for Memory Failure

I had not spoken to my friend for a few days, so I had not been reminded about the dinner. My wife also forgot and I tend to rely on her for social arrangements. (So really, it was her fault!)   *Anon.*

Solution

Forgetting a dinner engagement appears to be a fairly common experience. It is sensible for the host to cue the guests on the day of the dinner, as well as for partners to discuss their future dinner engagements. An obvious reminder for dinner engagements is to keep a calendar where it will be frequently seen. Better still, use a personal data assistant that will automatically sound an alarm before you have to get ready for social visits.

17. Forgetting My *Palmtop Computer*

In spring 1997 I gave a lecture on technology to a group of teachers at a hotel. At the beginning of the talk I placed my Sharp Wizard®, a palmtop computer used to aid memory, next to the projector that I used for overhead transparencies. I had programmed into this device a series of beeps to warn me when I had finished each section of the talk. The screen of the device also showed keywords to remind me of what I was to talk about in the next section. I was clearly technologically sophisticated: I was talking about technology while being aided by a device to help me remember.

After I had presented my lecture, one person came up and we talked about technology and teaching for about 20 minutes. I packed my papers and transparencies as we talked because I had to leave shortly afterward. About 2 hours later, while I was in the taxi to the airport, I realized that my Wizard® was back at the hotel, probably next to the overhead projector. I used the Wizard® frequently, so its absence reminded me that I had left it behind. Apart from containing all of my appointments for the next 6 months, the Wizard® cost $240. From more than one angle, I did not want to lose it.

When I reached the airport, I called the people at the hotel. They found the Wizard® where I had left it and, for a few dollars, mailed it back to me.

Reasons for Memory Failure

This was another case of distraction caused by being involved in other activities. I forgot the Wizard® because I was occupied answering questions and discussing various details with the person who came up after my talk. I then also failed to institute checking procedures, i.e. checking that everything had been collected before leaving.   *D.H.*

Solution

Once again it is clear that after every distraction it is essential to go through checking procedures to ensure that you take with you everything that you brought. It is a good idea to keep all valuables on your person, e.g. the Wizard® should have been put back in a pocket after use.

18. Leaving My Coat after a *Memory Improvement Lecture*

Herb Weingartner invited me to lecture on memory improvement at George Washington University. Since it was chilly that morning when I left, I wore my naval jacket. On arrival, Herb told me to hang my coat on a hook behind the door in his office.

We talked for a couple hours and then I gave my lecture. Afterwards we went out to buy some sandwiches. The weather had warmed up and it had turned out to be a nice spring day. I thanked Herb for inviting me and then I went to catch a train on the Underground.

I had travelled five stops when I realized that my coat was still in his office. I considered returning but decided against it, because it would take too much time. I returned to work and called Herb to arrange to get my coat back.

Reasons for Memory Failure

This was a classic case of multi-causal memory failure. I forgot my coat because the cues to remember it had vanished:

- By putting the coat behind a door, I could no longer see it and the change in the weather from cold to warm eliminated my need for a coat.

- I was tired after giving the lecture and the continual conversation with Herb and colleagues distracted me from thoughts about my coat. *D.H.*

Solution

Although similar in some ways to the previous incident, this failure also involves a vanishing cue. Vanishing cues refer to situations where a cue (reminder) that was present vanishes. This can happen when something blocks your view of a cue that would normally remind you to take something with you. Doors can close, covering things you want to remember. Vanishing cues are, of course, extremely difficult for anyone to do anything about. However, some vanishing cues are more likely to vanish from sight than others, e.g. if you hang up your coat behind a door when visiting a restaurant, you should be aware that the cue will vanish. Therefore, make a mental reminder to ask for the coat before you leave.

Certain possessions are more vulnerable than others to vanishing-cue situations. Umbrellas turn out not to be needed because of a change in the weather, and rain stopping is a vanishing cue. Jackets in spring are often taken off and laid aside, to vanish from sight – and mind – when the weather turns warm.

19. Plant *Murder*

I like my plants but I rarely remember to water them before they are wilted – or worse.

Reasons for Memory Failure

I forget to water the plants because:

- I see them every day and therefore come to pay less attention to them and how they look.

- The intervals between watering are long and are different for different plants, which makes it hard to remember.

- Plants are not a high priority. *H.M.*

Solution

This kind of forgetting is insidious. By the time there is a physical cue, such as a wilting plant, it is often too late to save it. In the case of plants there is a large interval of time during which it is optimal to water, and, indeed, too much watering can be fatal. One solution to the problem is to buy a plant alarm that beeps when the soil becomes too dry.

Of course, many people are devoted to their houseplants and manage them successfully without any help. This suggests that failing to water plants to the extent that they keep dying might have a great deal to do with a lack of motivation to care for them. The solution in such a case is simple – *let them die*!

20. Forgetting to *Load the Suitcase*

Rhona, my wife, and I had booked to go for a weekend break to Cambridge, some 5 hours drive from Swansea. Rhona had packed the case and left it in the hall. We made sure the children were all seen to and started on our journey to Cambridge. At about Newport, some 80 miles (128 kilometres) down the road, I asked Rhona if she had put the case in the car. She said 'No'; she thought I had done it, since this was the only thing I had to do!

I stopped the car and looked in the luggage compartment. The case was not there and we had to drive all the way back to Swansea to collect it. The journey back was filled with stimulating conversation. It was also filled with long periods without any conversation at all!

Reasons for Memory Failure

Quite clearly communication between my wife and I had broken down. I assumed my wife had loaded the case because she is always responsible for everything to do with travel and holiday arrangements. She assumed I had loaded the case because I had nothing else to do and she thought I would have helped by doing at least this. Because we were both so confident that the other had carried out the task we did not remind each other by asking about the case.

M.G.

Solution

If the suitcase had been placed in a prominent place by my wife (or me), e.g. just beside the door, then it would have acted as a physical cue. It was therefore a failure to ensure physical cues that led to the memory failure. It is always a good idea to leave anything that you should take out of the house in a prominent place so that it will automatically cue you when you leave the premises. This example also shows that it is good to talk to your spouse!

A frequent memory failure is to leave an article, such as a book or a present, at home or at work rather than to take it to a friend or colleague.

1. To remember to take something with you when you leave home, keep a table or chair near the door and place the object on this as soon as it is ready. This will prompt your memory as soon as you go out of the door.

2. The solution is the same at work. Leave a chair by the door where you can place your briefcase or files if you need to take them with you when you go.

21. Coffee Mugs and *Car Roofs*

I usually take a cup of coffee with me to drink as I drive to work. My mug has a wide, flat bottom so it can sit on the dashboard and not slide about. I customarily put the mug on top of the car while I open the back door and put my briefcase inside.

One particular morning I put my cup on top of the car and then discovered that my wife had parked her car pretty close to mine. I could only open the front or back door of the car partially but managed to manoeuvre my briefcase around the back door and onto the back seat. Perhaps a little annoyed, I then scrunched myself up so that I could squeeze into the front seat. I backed out of the garage, closed the garage door with the remote car-door opener and backed out of the drive onto the street.

After throwing the car into first and second gear, I reached for my coffee. When I saw my mug was not on the dashboard, I felt for it on the passenger seat since I sometimes put the cup there. Then I had an 'ah-ha, oh no' experience: I realized that the cup was still on top of the car.

Our house is on one of the busier thoroughfares so I immediately thought: 'Oh no. I have got to get that cup off the car before someone who knows me passes by and sees me.' I pulled the car over immediately and, sticking my arm out the car window, reached up for the cup, which amazingly was where I had left it on the roof. Fortunately, no colleague passed by (to the best of my knowledge) but quite a few neighbours saw me. I could imagine what they were thinking!

Reasons for Memory Failure

I forgot I had put the cup on the car roof for a couple of good reasons:

- There was little space between the cars and I had to bend over low to manoeuvre myself into the front seat. This process

| Memory Hints | **Remembering Items on the Car Roof** |

Our investigations suggest that leaving things on the roof of a car is quite a common memory failure. It probably happens because the roof is the right height at which to place things when getting into a car and, after opening a car door, you are often distracted at the point of getting in.

These really are 'bad luck' failures in many cases and highlight the need to be aware, when entering a car, that you should check that nothing is left on the roof (or anywhere else!) after any distraction.

distracted me from remembering that I had put my mug on top of the car.

- Because I had to scrunch up to get into the car, I was no longer able to see the cup, so – out of sight, out of mind. Previously when I have got into the car without the cup I have been reminded of it because I naturally see it on the roof.

One way of looking at this memory failure is to blame my wife for parking so close. Had she not done so, I would not have had to stoop to get into the car and I would have caught myself making the error!   *D.H.*

Solution

Spouses are clearly a major source of memory failures:

- They fail to remind us of things when we are depending on them.
- They are a constant source of distraction by annoying us in various ways.

The best way to avoid the latter is to keep them happy, then they will not annoy you. A happy partner equals a good memory! (Plenty of reminders and less distraction from arguments.)

22. Forgetting My *Bank Number*

Being a memory expert, I use a memory system to remember numbers, such as birthdays, anniversaries, telephone numbers and bank personal identification numbers (PINs). It is a system that has worked very well in the past and I used it for remembering my bank PIN the first time I was given it. However, it was some time between my using the PIN for the first time and needing to use it a second time and, needless to say, I forgot the number when I needed to use it again. I tried three times and the cash machine would not return my card. It was, to say the least, an embarrassing experience for a so-called memory expert!

Reasons for Memory Failure

A major reason was over-confidence that the memory system which I used was perfect. It is very good, but, if the material is not used for some time, you can forget. One memory failure such as this does not mean that memory systems are useless in helping you to remember numbers. They are usually very good indeed, provided the memory is refreshed from time to time. When I have done this with a new PIN, I remember it perfectly.

M.G.

Solution

One solution is to put your PIN in your diary, or personal data assistant if you have one, adding bogus numbers in case the information falls into the wrong hands. You can also put half the numbers in one place and the rest in another. A better solution for many people is to make sure you carry the numbers around in your head. (For an account of the Digit Letter Memory System, which is designed to help you remember numbers such as PINs, see p. 93.)

23. Mistaking the *Sex of our Cat*

We bought a new female cat, called 'Ginger,' for our daughter, Mandy, early for Christmas. Nearly a month later we took the cat to the vet for vaccinations. The vet informed her that the cat was male, not female. By this time, Mandy was attached to the cat and decided to keep it, even though it was male.

In the ensuing days, each of us – Mandy, my wife Donna, and myself – had tremendous difficulty remembering Ginger's sex. We repeatedly called him 'her' or 'she'.

Reasons for Memory Failure

The sex of an animal is such a fundamental concept that it was not easy to overcome the wrong sex information. There are not many cues (apart from the obvious one, which requires observation from a particular perspective!) as to the sex of a cat so, in the absence of a physical cue, old habits will sometimes dominate when there is a lack of concentration. A cat is not as important as a human being – so the taboo about confusing the sex of a cat is far less than for a human being.

D.H.

Solution

The solution to this kind of problem is not to worry about it. Many memory failures are not worth worrying about and just because you have more failures as you get older does not mean that you are losing your marbles. We all have memory failures at all ages.

24. Which Motel *Are We Staying At?*

I took my 10-year-old son, Zachary, with me on a visit to Chicago. I had to work before we left and we did not leave for Chicago until after supper. We drove until it was late (for a 10-year-old) to the outskirts of Chicago, stopped at about midnight and checked into a motel. By then I was as tired as he was and we fell fast asleep immediately.

In the morning we drove into the heart of Chicago. My son was very well behaved. We went to the Museum of Science and Industry and had a great time, going into the coal-mine, looking at the exhibits concerning medicine and a host of other things. We went to a restaurant for dinner, and shared a lot of 'men's' talk.

After dinner we set off along the motorway for our motel. However, as we approached the general region of the motel, I realized that I had not noted the exit which I needed to take in order to get to it. I drove east for 15 minutes, then west for 15 minutes. I carefully studied the exit signs but they did not help. I actually did not even know what town the motel was in. Zachary began to complain that it was taking awfully long to reach the motel and I became worried. Our suitcases and clothes were at the motel. What would I tell my wife if I had lost a bunch of clothes because I forgot which motel we were staying at? She has had more than enough experience of my unfortunate memory failures to allow me to blame it on my son.

Finally, I narrowed the possible exits down to three. I took the first but quickly realized that it was not the right one: there were no motels there. I went back onto the motorway and took the next likely exit and, as I left the motorway, I saw our motel. Thank heavens! Although the motel had been obscured by trees on the motorway, I was very grateful that Zachary did not know that his father was lost.

Reasons for Memory Failure

I forgot the location of the motel for a number of reasons:

- Because I was tired on arrival, I checked in without noting my surroundings.
- My mind was on what I had to do the next day, so I did not notice the number of the nearest motorway exit.
- Although my spatial relations are generally pretty good, at least in a small town, I had forgotten how hard it is to find your way around a big city like Chicago.
- The trees obscured the motel from the motorway, denying me any visual cues.

D.H.

As noted before (p. 18), travelling plays havoc with your memory, not only because of the stress involved, but because much of the context is new and strange, and does not provide the normal memory prompts. Nevertheless, there are a number of things that can be done to make life easier.

1. Packing

Very commonly, when people unpack their suitcase on arriving at their holiday destination, they find that shirts, underpants, toiletries or bathing suits have been forgotten. There then follows half an hour of recriminations while blame is allocated. This normally takes the form of the person who is regarded as responsible for packing, denying responsibility for the other person's goods, or arguing that the stress of attending to this and looking after that was just too great without help! One solution is for the parties to get together beforehand to list what needs to be packed and to agreed how this should happen. The list should then be ticked off as items are packed.

2. Travel Necessities

As well as suitcases, it is advisable, as noted earlier (p. 18), to make a checklist of all travel necessities: tickets, money, passports, etc. But, as the experiences of both D.H. and M.G. clearly illustrate, it is not enough to check that you have them. Passports should be checked at least 2 months before departure to ensure that they are not out of date. Tickets should be checked at least a week in advance and then the day before to ensure that you do not turn up to the wrong airport (D.H., p. 42), a day early (M.G, p. 18), or, worse still, an hour late!

Solution

People are very vulnerable to memory failure when travelling because the context (where a hotel is, its surroundings, etc.) are all new. It is always a good idea to write down the name and address of a hotel when checking in and to pay particular attention to important surrounding landmarks.

25. The Elevator Cue Problem: *Right or Left?*

One government building I used to work in was designed by an architect who was either mean or had a great sense of humour. The foyer on every floor of the building looked exactly the same, whether you arrived in the east elevator or the west elevator. The marble, the buttons, even the ashtrays, were positioned in exactly the same way. When I was new to the job, I would find myself leaving the elevator and turning left when I should have turned right – or right when I should have turned left.

Of course, I was correct half the time but it was the errors I made during the other half that I found embarrassing. I discovered that I could avoid this embarrassment if I always stood in the back of the elevator. Then I could observe which way one of the veteran employees turned and would not turn the wrong way.

However, watching the veteran employees was not foolproof because even they made mistakes and would watch each other when leaving the elevator. It was as if everyone in the elevator lingered a little longer before getting out in order to avoid making a mistake. The most obvious solution to this dilemma was to deface the foyers in some distinguishable way, but that was a federal offence. A more realistic solution was to take note of whether you went up on the east elevator or the west elevator and to remember 'When east go right and when west go left'. The disorientation caused by these identical foyers probably interfered with the completion of many federal projects, costing taxpayers a great deal of money!

Reasons for Memory Failure

Along with many other people, I do not normally try to remember whether I have taken the east or west elevator and foyers are rarely designed to look identical. There were very few methods which I could use to ensure that I took the correct direction when leaving the elevator.   *D.H.*

Solution

The only solution to this problem would be to realize its insidious nature and pay much more attention to which elevator you were taking. Fortunately, this is not a common problem. It is uncanny how D.H. seems to experience this so regularly!

26. Lost *Lock Combinations*

Over the years, my children and I have engaged sporadically in sporting activities, especially swimming. These involve changing into sports clothes and putting your street clothes into a locker. Because my street clothes contain my wallet, I purchased a combination lock to put on the locker.

Unfortunately, we have not engaged in athletic activity very often. Equally unfortunately, I have not been in a habit of copying down the combination to the lock or I have lost the piece of paper with the combination on it. As a result, I now have a small collection of combination locks that I do not know how to open. I do not know why I keep them – unless I harbour a desire to humiliate myself into keeping better records of lock combinations in the future!

Reasons for Memory Failure

Numbers are difficult to remember at the best of times and I clearly did not make enough effort to remember them in the first place or to write them down.   *D.H.*

Solution

Writing down numbers, such as combination lock numbers or bank PINs, is only useful if you do not lose the original numbers. If you do write important numbers down, disguise them in some way and do not carry them in the same place as your credit card. Alternatively, use the Digit Letter Memory System to remember any sequence of numbers that is important to you. However, remember that no method is infallible (p. 93).

27. Which Airport *Was It?*

In the winter of 1995 I applied for several jobs and was invited to an interview for a position at Indiana State University. I did not want to advertise to my current employer that I was looking for another job so my travel agent arranged for me to catch a flight to Indianapolis after work. There someone was to pick me up and drive me on to the university at Terre Haute.

The travel agent posted my ticket to me a few weeks before the day of the interview. On the day of travelling I left work promptly at 4.30 p.m. and drove to Washington National airport. The traffic was not too bad so I arrived there at 5.30 p.m. Washington National was my favourite Washington airport, as Dulles and Baltimore/Washington airports were both quite a distance from where I worked.

When I arrived at Washington National, I parked and took out my ticket to see which airline I was travelling with. I went into shock as I read my ticket, which said that I was flying from Baltimore/Washington airport. My pulse raced. Baltimore/Washington was at least another hour away from Washington National. I had even less time to make the flight than if I had gone directly to Baltimore/Washington airport from work. Fortunately, as my ticket showed, my flight did not leave until 7.30 p.m.

I jumped back into my car and drove as fast as traffic would allow. However, it was the rush hour, so even if I had wanted to speed, I did not have much opportunity to do so. I figured that I was probably going to miss the flight and imagined calling the person from Indiana State University who was going to pick me up at 11.30 p.m. from Indianapolis airport. I tried to think of an excuse I could offer for missing my flight but none seemed good enough and it seemed likely that I would not get the job.

I arrived at Baltimore/Washington airport at about 7.10 p.m., parked in the first car-park I could find and looked for a taxi. I could not find one, so I caught the airport bus – taking more time. When I arrived at the airline desk, they told me to run and called ahead to hold the door. Amazingly, I made the flight and arrived at Indianapolis on time, cool as a cucumber.

It was a good interview. I liked them and they liked me. They offered me the job and I took it. The job turned out to be great and Indiana State is a great place to be. I cannot believe how close I came to blowing it.

Reasons for Memory Failure

I went to Washington National airport instead of Baltimore/Washington airport because:

- I habitually flew from Washington National.

- The flight arrangements were made nearly a month before the flight.

- With so much time, I forgot that the agent had switched me to Baltimore/Washington so that I would get to Indianapolis in time.

- I did not check my tickets and relied instead on my excellent memory. Checking tickets arouses my anxiety so I avoid doing so until I get to the airport (a bad practice).   *D.H.*

Solution

This failure has a great deal in common with earlier failures involving travel where there was a failure to check flight details.

Over-confidence in the correctness of your memory can override checking procedures. You must not put yourself in a mental state in which you are absolutely certain that you are correct. Indeed one of the most frequently reported results in eyewitness research is a lack of any major relationship between eyewitness confidence and eyewitness accuracy.

Where the cost of a memory mistake is high, it is always worth checking, as the contents of this book frequently show. A good check for people who are travelling is to look over the tickets and related materials the night before travelling.

28. Photographs for the *Memory Book*

Before going to work abroad for a year, I arranged for someone to photograph drawings of famous philosophers from previous centuries. I needed the photographs in order to meet a deadline with the publisher of my first book, which was about how people have explained memory throughout history. About 2 days after I picked up the photos, I prepared an envelope so that I could send them to the publisher. However, I could no longer find the photos, which had been in my hands just 2 days before.

I panicked. I went through every file in my filing cabinets but, after hours of searching, I just could not find the photos. I suspected that someone had accidentally thrown them away. I went back to the photographer and begged him to make another set of photos. He eventually agreed to do so but was clearly angry about my loss of the original set that he had slaved over. When I returned from abroad, I found the photos in a folder that was appropriately labelled 'Figures for the Historical Book'. When I found the folder, I remembered having put the photos there.

Reasons for Memory Failure

I forgot where I put the photographs because:

- Our house was in chaos prior to my leaving for the sabbatical.
- I made the mistake of storing them in a place that was rarely used. It is common for people to store valuables in a 'safe' place and to forget where that safe place is, and this is true for people of all ages. If the storage takes place when you have a lot of distractions, as in this case, or when there is a long time gap between the storing and trying to find what was stored, the problem is obviously greater. *D.H.*

Solution

The advantages of a well-organized filing system or storing items in one of a number of places you will easily remember are obvious.

29. Forgetting the Way to a *New Destination*

I had to attend a regular class at the National Institute of Health Clinical Center. Because this building follows a haphazard design, I sometimes forgot the way from the entrance to the classroom.

Reasons for Memory Failure

This often happens when driving a car on a road which is familiar, but where you have to turn off at a junction which is unusual for you. The strongly established habit predominates, aided probably by distraction, such as thinking of another important task or talking to someone.

A professor of our acquaintance once went back to his old house after he had sold it, sat in his usual place in the kitchen and only realized his mistake when he found that the newspaper he was reading was the 'wrong' one. I forgot the way because finding your way is a boring task. I was typically thinking about other things. Some people have great difficulty in learning routes when on holiday, possibly because they do not take the trouble to learn the layout properly in the first place. *D.H.*

Solution

Failing to remember directions, even of familiar routes and buildings, is a common experience. This is probably because most people assume that

1. Special Places

We have all experienced misplacing items. Sometimes this happens because we want to hide valuables away when we leave the house and so put things in a special place which we cannot later remember. This can be avoided by having a limited number of 'special' places in which you place your valuables. Thus you will be much less likely to forget where you put something.

2. Retracing Your Steps

Often misplacing items is much more mundane: we cannot remember where we put our car keys or house keys. Again, having one place to put the keys when entering the house helps greatly, but we still sometimes misplace items. When this happens, stay calm and *retrace* your steps from the last time you definitely remember having the item. What happened next? Did the phone ring, etc.? What events might have distracted you? What were you thinking about? What rooms did you go in? Did you give the missing item to anyone? It often helps to go into each room in turn. Sometimes the new context helps to prompt you, e.g. the telephone off the hook might remind you that you were in the room with your keys and gave them to your brother.

3. Memory Blocks

Sometimes when you have such a memory failure, you should try for a long time to think about where the missing item should be, then stop thinking about it for a bit, say an hour or two, before trying again. When you stop trying to remember, the memory block sometimes dissipates so that, when you try again, the memory comes back.

they will remember and consequently do not make the effort to work out the layout of a route or building. Often you are talking to someone else when you are using a route for the first time, or thinking about the purpose of the visit. Often forgetting a route is not a great problem because you can usually ask the way. On occasion it can be serious, e.g. when you end up in a rough area of a city.

The solution is to be aware of the problem and to make a conscious effort to remember landmarks, study maps and write down directions beforehand. If someone is giving you verbal directions, do not be too proud to write them down because you may not be capable of absorbing all the information.

Annoying or **Inconveniencing Others**

Memory failures are worse when they cause annoyance to others. Too many memory failures at work, for example, could result in you being fired.

30. Going to the *Wrong House*

I had been drinking heavily at a party and it was time to go home. Just 3 days before, we had moved to another house which was fairly close to the one we had left. At 2.00 a.m. I went to my old house, tried my keys, but the door would not open. I thought the door had been locked accidentally from the inside, so I banged on the door to get in. When someone eventually opened it, I was highly embarrassed to realize my mistake.

Reasons for Memory Failure

Alcohol had undoubtedly affected my ability to think and remember. The fact that the two houses, my old and my new one, were quite close together meant that, by not thinking, I failed to notice that I was taking the route to my old house. Alcohol causes memory failure because it interferes with the ability both to process new information and to take in and process important social and physical prompts.   *J.M.*

Solution

Do not drink too much if you move houses!

31. You Can't Think of Everything *When Locking Your Car!*

I routinely locked my car when working in Washington DC. One day, I got out of the car and put my keys in my overcoat pocket instead of my trouser pocket. I walked a few steps and decided it was too warm to wear my overcoat. I unlocked the car, returned my keys to my overcoat pocket, threw my coat into the back seat of the car and shut the car door. When I arrived at the building where I worked, I looked for my keys and realized that I had locked them in the car. I called Donna, my wife, and she came (an hour's drive from home) and unlocked my car.

Reasons for Memory Failure

Locking your key inside your car is one of the most common memory failures and one of the most frustrating. It was common for me to put my keys in my coat once I got in the office. Unfortunately, this time I put my keys in my coat *before* I got to the office!   *D.H.*

Solution

Always carry a spare car key! If you are distracted when you get out of your car, either by someone or by something, always check before you leave that you have not left the keys in the ignition. A good idea is always to look at your keys in your hand when you take them out of the ignition. If you can afford it, buy a car that sounds an alarm when you leave your keys in the ignition. Never put keys on a seat or anywhere else but in your pocket or purse.

32. But You Can Check that the *Car Is Really Locked!*

One day in spring, I got out of the car and put my keys in my overcoat pocket instead of my trouser pocket. I walked a few steps and decided it was too warm to wear my overcoat. I unlocked the car, returned my keys to my overcoat pocket, threw my coat into the back seat of the car and shut the car door. At the end of the day I left work and discovered, when I got to the car, that I had again locked my keys inside. I checked the doors and could see that they were locked.

I called Donna, my wife, and asked if she could come and unlock the car. Unfortunately, she couldn't come because of other responsibilities. I called the American Automobile Association (AAA), who agreed to come in a couple of hours. When the locksmith arrived, he unlocked the car door on the front passenger's side. When he opened it, he motioned that I could now reach in and open the other doors. When I reached into the back and attempted to unlock the back door, I discovered that it had been unlocked all along. Apparently I did not look closely enough earlier in the day when I decided that I was locked out. The AAA call-out cost me $25. I did not have the nerve to tell the locksmith that his work had been unnecessary all along!

Reasons for Memory Failure

I locked my keys in the car because I put the keys in my coat pocket and made the mistake of putting my coat in the car. When you have one memory failure, you may well become distracted and upset, making the chances of another memory failure more likely. Thus I not only deviated from my routine of putting my keys in my trouser pocket but also didn't check carefully enough to see if any door was unlocked.   *D.H.*

Solution

Try to learn from previous mistakes.

Causing Damage

Even worse than causing inconvenience to others is causing actual physical damage. In one of the following examples the physical damage was to the person who had the memory failure! However, causing actual damage as a result of memory failure can be a very serious problem: many car and air crashes are caused by memory failures at critical times.

33. Zip-fasteners Can *Damage Your Health!*

One evening my wife and I went to a party. It was going very well and everyone was enjoying themselves. I had to go to the bathroom and, being in a hurry to get back to the party, unfortunately forgot to replace my manhood before I pulled up my zip-fastener. The latter caught in the former and caused excruciating pain. Also, the more I tried to undo the zip-fastener, the more it hurt. The bathroom door remained locked for about a quarter of an hour while I struggled in great pain. The other guests were banging on the bathroom door and shouting.

Reasons for Memory Failure

I was distracted by wanting to get back to the party but I have to admit that even 3-year-olds manage to perform the action that I failed to perform with greater competence. However, it was such a painful experience that I have not repeated it since. A classic case of instant learning!   *M.G.*

Solution

Do what M.G. did just once. You will never do it again!

34. Forgetting the *Fuel Hose*

A friend visited me to discuss some work we were doing together and we talked incessantly for hours. I then remembered that I had to get fuel in order to take him to the airport the next day. I went to the fuel station while he continued our work and, putting the hose in the fuel intake, set the catch to fill it automatically.

I went into the store to buy a snack. When I came out, I could see from a distance that the meter showed the fuel pump had stopped, indicating my car was full up. I went back into the store to pay for the fuel.

After paying for the fuel, I got into the car, started the engine and began to leave the station. I was probably doing about 5–10 miles per hour (10–15 kilometres per hour) when, suddenly, there was a loud bang and the car stopped momentarily. I looked behind me, thinking that someone had run into me.

Instead I saw someone in the car behind waving wildly at me, so I got out of the car to see what I had done. The fuel hose was hanging from my car, having been ripped off the pump. I went back into the store and gave the assistant my address, telling him to send me the bill. He was furious. He said that I was an idiot and I had to agree with him. I returned the next day and the manager said that the company would pay for the hose. He also reassured me, saying that I was not the first person to drive away with a pump!

Reasons for Memory Failure

Going to buy food meant that I no longer saw the fuel hose. Normally this would not matter too much but, when combined with the distraction of thinking about the work I was doing with my friend and my fatigue, the memory failure was inevitable. *D.H.*

Solution

This was a classic case of distraction and preoccupation. Being aware that this is when memory failures are likely to occur is the first step towards proper checking procedures. But mistakes like this can happen to any overworked memory expert. However, like the mistake with the zip-fastener, make this mistake once and you will not make it again! As a general rule you should not leave machinery, including fuel pumps, until the operation is finished.

35. Forgetting to Turn *Off the Water Taps*

One morning when I was working in Russia, the water supply was turned off at 8.00 a.m. (while I was filling the bath). I finished my bath and left for the day. Unfortunately, I forgot to turn off the taps and, when the water came on again, it flooded flats for three floors below!

Reasons for Memory Failure

This is a classic case of the disappearance of a physical cue. Had the water been running, this would have been a physical cue for me to turn off the taps. It is difficult to regard this as a memory 'fault' as opposed to a memory failure – but tell that to those who lived in the flats below!

Anon.

Solution

This is just one of those things. There is no real solution. However, just as in the last example, when you finish something, you should finish it completely or stop. Never leave bath taps running in case you are distracted and water floods the house. If you must attend to something else, turn the taps off.

Similarly, when you have finished cooking, turn off the burners. It is never a good idea to leave something to cook while you leave the house to go visiting. Almost everyone has had the experience of being delayed, or staying away much longer than planned, when they have left something on the cooker.

36. Car-reversing *Memory Failures*

While I am a reasonably good driver, with a reasonably good record going forward, my reversing does seem to leave a lot to be desired. On one occasion, when I was newly arrived as a lecturer in Swansea, a highly respected senior colleague, who had just bought a new car, parked directly behind my old Bedford van. When I reversed my van, I forgot to look in the rear-view mirror. I reversed into my colleague's new car, damaging its front. Clearly it was an embarrassing experience.

Reasons for Memory Failure

I was thinking of other things when I should have looked in the mirror.

M.G.

 Solution

Failing to look in the mirror is a frequent cause of accidents. Always be aware that reversing is a dangerous procedure. You *must* look in the mirror before you reverse.

Appearing Dishonest

Possibly one of the most serious consequences of memory failure, and one which many of us dread, is being thought dishonest because we have forgotten to pay for goods. It is clear from the examples below that this has happened to many people and it presents society with a major problem: how to take account of honest people forgetting while at the same time preventing dishonest people from stealing. What the following examples show is that we all have the potential to be caught in a situation of forgetting to pay and that we are particularly vulnerable if we have major problems on our mind. Knowing when we are vulnerable is likely to go some, but not all, of the way to dealing with the problem.

37. Failing to *Pay for Fuel*

Some time ago I had a lot going on at work. Things were going well; in particular I was a senior organizer of the First International Conference on Practical Aspects of Memory. This required me to travel to Cardiff, some 40 miles (65 kilometres) from my home town of Swansea. I filled up my car with fuel, thinking all the time about the problems I had to deal with, and then drove off without paying. During the drive back from Cardiff, I suddenly realized that I had not paid for the fuel. I drove back to the fuel station and paid immediately. The attendant remarked that he had noticed that I looked preoccupied.

Reasons for Memory Failure

Clearly the main reason I forgot to pay was because my work weighed heavily on my mind. Six months later I again forgot to pay but did not remember. I received a 'friendly' call, suggesting I get down to the garage 'pretty quick' or I would be prosecuted. I believe I was saved from prosecution because of the previous incident, so the proprietors knew I was honest, if forgetful.

Indeed a society has been formed in the UK of individuals who believe themselves to be wrongly convicted of shoplifting. Professor James

Reason, who investigated the members' cases, found that in many instances there had been a traumatic incident, such as a bereavement or serious accident in the family, in the 3–6 months previous to the conviction.

Of course, shoplifting has many causes and genuine forgetting is only one of these. Clearly, too, a defence of forgetting cannot be accepted uncritically or everyone would just walk out of shops with goods without paying. However, it is quite clear that genuinely forgetting to pay for goods is a very common phenomenon and, if justice is to be done, it must be properly investigated in every case where it has possibly occurred.

M.G.

 ## Solution

This is undoubtedly one of the most distressing memory failures because it can lead to a criminal conviction. Such failures happen to people who are extremely preoccupied and, as noted above, many people who have had a major traumatic experience in the prior 6 months seem to have been wrongly convicted. On the other hand, as M.G.'s failure to pay for fuel showed, it can just be due to preoccupation with on-going events.

There is no foolproof way of preventing this from happening, but you must be aware that over-preoccupation with your problems can lead to difficulties when shopping and buying goods. You *must* tell yourself to pay attention to the world, but it is not always easy.

However, if you have made this kind of mistake you must rectify it as soon as possible. You must never be too embarrassed to go back and admit the mistake.

38. Signing *Credit-card Slips*

A certain kind of forgetting recurs in my life, despite the fact that this forgetting is embarrassing and annoying. When at a store I often use my credit card. I hand the card over and talk to the assistant while waiting for my credit status to be approved electronically. However, many stores in our locality give their own receipt as well as presenting the credit-card slip for signature. Other stores do not give their own receipt and only provide the credit-card slip.

My problem is that, when I am in stores which give both receipts, I sometimes attempt to walk out with the merchandise as soon as I have been given the store receipt but without signing the credit-card slip. When the conversation between myself and the assistant seems to have reached an appropriate end, I automatically say 'Thank you' and start to leave, unless the assistant also automatically says 'You still have to sign your credit-card slip'. Depending on how you want to view this event, it could appear that I am trying to get away without paying for what I have got at the store. Even if my honesty is not impugned, my behaviour certainly looks suspicious to the assistant and other customers waiting to be served.

Reasons for Memory Failure

I make this failure for two reasons:

- The conversation with the assistant requires mental effort and this mental activity makes me forget the credit-card transaction.

- Because some stores give just one receipt, I automatically conclude that the transaction has ended as soon as I am given the store receipt. *D.H.*

Solution

Clearly, it would be extremely helpful if all stores used the same system. Then everyone would get into the same routine. The end of a purchase used to be a receipt. Now it is usually a receipt *and* a credit-card slip. Remember to wait for both.

39. Forgetting to Pay *in a Supermarket*

When my daughter was a baby, I used to feed her grapes in supermarkets to keep her quiet. These made a mess and required a bib to save her clothes. I often forgot to bring a bib, so I would take one out of a packet in the shop. Unfortunately, I sometimes forgot to take the opened packet to the check-out.

Reasons for Memory Failure

Mothers with babies have a number of built-in memory problems, such as lack of sleep resulting in lack of concentration and attention, the often urgent demands of babies requiring immediate attention, the many things to think about when looking after baby and the household. It is not surprising that memory failures of the kind described above occur.

Anon.

Solution

Obviously when you have a young child, the energy you use up is likely to result in memory problems for a number of reasons:

- Children must be attended to immediately in case the problem is urgent and so other less important matters are forgotten.

- Tiredness leads to memory problems and new mothers have to deal with a range of emotional and hormonal adjustments, which are likely to preoccupy them, resulting in memory problems.

- Pain and depression, where it occurs, can cause memory problems.

Usually problems caused by putting children first are unimportant. In stores, however, it is essential to be more aware than usual of the possibility of memory failure.

Appearing **Foolish**

Almost all memory failures can make us feel foolish, so to some extent the selection of memory-failure episodes in this section, as, indeed, in other sections, is somewhat arbitrary. However, most of the examples here did not have very serious consequences. They just left the perpetrators feeling that they could have handled things better!

40. **Forgetting to** *Wear A Tie*

I made an appointment to meet my immediate boss and her boss to discuss serious matters pertaining to management. At the meeting I made an impassioned plea for a change in procedure. My bosses listened to me patiently for at least 20 minutes and we talked afterward for another half an hour. I thanked them for their time and left.

A few minutes later, someone asked why I was not wearing a tie, which was customary where I worked. I quickly escaped to my office and put on the tie which I keep in my drawer for such an occasion. (I have done this since I once left the house but realized I had forgotten my tie well before I got to work. Fortunately, I had enough time to return home and fetch one.)

Reasons for Memory Failure

Obviously, meeting your boss over a 'serious matter' is stressful for anyone and leads to mental overload i.e. thinking in too focused a way about the meeting ahead to the exclusion of other necessary matters. In this organization, formality was a high priority, so failing to wear a tie and to pick up cues that I was not wearing a tie were, in this context, major memory failures. The lack of cues obviously did not help the memory process.

D.H.

Solution

Obviously wearing a tie presents memory problems to memory experts. M.G. once forgot he was already wearing a tie and put on a second tie to go for an interview with his professor! One solution is always to check your appearance in a mirror before an important appointment. It is a good idea to keep a tie in your glove compartment, in your briefcase or in your office.

41. Forgetting the *Oil-cap*

In spring 1986, Donna, Mandy and I were touring Scotland with Matt, Wendy and Josh Weber. We had been travelling together for a few days and, although Donna and Wendy knew each other to some extent, the rest of us did not know each other at all. Consequently, everyone was trying hard to establish a friendly relationship.

Everything had been going along well. We pulled into a fuel station in a small Scottish town to fill up both cars. I had to put oil in our car and, while doing so, I chatted with Matt and Wendy until our car was ready.

We then drove off in the direction of the next town on our itinerary. However, within a few minutes, the reading on our car's thermometer shot up, indicating that the engine was overheating. Smoke began to pour from beneath the bonnet. Then the car began to run more and more slowly until it finally stopped. We pulled off the side of the road and called the Royal Automobile Club (RAC).

When he arrived, the RAC mechanic looked under the bonnet, almost immediately noticed that someone had failed to replace the oil-cap and showed us that oil had spilled out all over the engine. When he commented that we would have the basis for a legitimate complaint about the attendant who put in the oil at the fuel station, I sheepishly volunteered that I had put in the oil. Then he left to get enough oil to fill the car's engine, cautioning us that the engine may have been ruined. Fortunately, the engine started once it had been given enough oil.

Reasons for Memory Failure

Clearly a major cause of this memory failure was distraction due to social interaction combined with a lack of motivation to check that the chores had been completed. Also, I had rested the oil-cap on the engine, where it looked much like the rest of the engine. So, not being mechanically minded, I was not visually prompted to replace the cap. Since many major accidents, e.g. aircraft accidents, are caused by failing to check that things have been put back properly, this can be a serious matter. In one recent case in Germany, a fatal accident was caused on a railway when tools were left on the track by repairmen, causing a derailment.   *D.H.*

Solution

For many people, distraction while dealing with car problems is a major source of memory failures. As noted previously, these can involve leaving keys in the car or forgetting to pay for fuel, forgetting to put the handbrake on or, as in this case, failing to replace the oil-cap. Generally, it is not wise to talk to others when carrying out important tasks. You should be very aware of how important it is to check every aspect of dealing with your car. Memory failures can kill.

42. Knocking before *Leaving a Room*

I was once apprenticed as an accountant. I was not good at the job and frequently made mistakes. (Indeed, major mistakes of mine were still being discovered years after I left!) I was frequently called into the senior partner's office and, on many occasions, he yelled about my incompetence. I found the whole situation extremely stressful. Once, after being given yet another dressing-down, I turned to leave the senior partner's office and knocked on the door to get *out*!

Reasons for Memory Failure

Severe stress commonly produces memory failures. Stage fright and anxiety about messing up exams often forces the poor performance you fear. It is important to reduce stress to manageable proportions, although, where there is no stress, performance may suffer just as much because you put no effort into trying to remember. In my case, when I saw the closed door (a cue), and clearly wanting to get out of my boss's office, I was too stressed to process the cue properly. Instinctively I knocked on the door to get out, when knocking is, of course, only appropriate prior to going in!

M.G.

Solution

Always try to keep calm by getting things in perspective. Ask yourself: 'What is the worst thing that could happen?' The more flustered we become, the less information we take in from the surroundings and the more failures occur. When flustered, fix on the top of a door or the edge of a ceiling. Take a deep breath and hold it until you have to release it. Once you have calmed down, you can return to trying to remember.

43. Disney *Woe*

Since Tony believes that EPCOT (Experimental Prototype Community of Tomorrow), in Florida, USA, should be an all-day, all-night adventure, I visited a few exhibits with him and then arranged to meet him for dinner. I took the shuttle to the car-park, looking forward to an afternoon of reading by the hotel pool. I went to where I was sure I had left the car – and couldn't find it!

After going up and down the row many times, I sent for a security guard who drove me around. He was most distressed that I could barely describe the car ('a kind of off-white 4-door') because we had hired it only 36 hours before. We finally found it but only because I recognized the Universal Tour ticket on the dashboard, left from Tony's solo excursion the previous day.

Reasons for Memory Failure

Forgetting where you have parked a hire car is a frequent occurrence, simply because you are not familiar with its appearance. Also, when I got out of the car in the morning, the rear of the car was exposed. When I returned in the afternoon, the attendants had parked another row of cars behind it, so that, from a visual standpoint, my car was parked in a different row than I remembered. *H.N.*

Memory Hints | **Hire Cars**

To make it easier to find where you have parked a hire car, you should take the following steps:

1. Make a mental or written note of the registration number. (To make remembering the number easier, see p. 94.)

2. Make a mental note of distinguishing features of the car or leave something, such as a large map, on the back seat or the dashboard, or a large bag on the rear parcel-shelf.

Solution

This memory failure was not surprising. It is, however, a good idea to make your hire car physically distinctive so that recognition is easier.

44. Was it Columbia or *Charlotte?*

In spring 1994 I had to attend a meeting in Columbia, South Carolina. I arranged to fly out on Friday night after work because I did not have to be there until Saturday afternoon. I went to Baltimore/Washington airport that Friday afternoon and boarded the aircraft to Columbia. My itinerary involved a stop-over in Atlanta, where I would get my final flight to Columbia. I left Baltimore/Washington at around 7 p.m. and arrived in Atlanta at 9 p.m.

I checked in at the counter for the next flight to Columbia and sat down to read. After I had been reading for a while, I heard the announcement: 'Now boarding for Columbia'. I sprang to my feet and joined the line of other passengers waiting to board. The airline representative checked my ticket and tore off the appropriate slip.

I was very relieved to get on the aircraft because it was about 9.30 p.m. and I was exhausted after working all day. The aircraft was a 'puddle-jumper', i.e. intended for short-haul, internal flights, and I had an enjoyable conversation with a fellow passenger. As we began to circle for landing, I remarked that I had never been to Columbia before. This passenger looked at me with astonishment and said the aircraft was landing in Charlotte, North Carolina. I said: '*Oh no*, you must be mistaken.' He replied that he certainly was not because he flew in and out of Charlotte all the time and could recognize the city from the air. He even pointed out his home.

I summoned the flight attendant, who treated the whole matter as very serious. He explained that, because the aircraft was so small and there were only four passengers, he did not check our tickets carefully and did not announce the destination. It was serious to me as well because I was now worried whether I would be able to get to my meeting on time. The airline assumed all responsibility for the error. They put me up over night in a hotel and arranged for me to catch a flight to Columbia in the morning. (It was too late to get a flight to Columbia from Charlotte by the time we arrived.) Despite this, one airline representative did say: 'How *did* you do this?' I made it to the meeting with a couple of hours to spare.

Reasons for Memory Failure

Being too relaxed can lead to not checking what seems obvious, in this case that the flight called was the correct one. There are several reasons why I made this mistake:

- I was exhausted.

- Flights for Columbia and Charlotte boarded from the same gate.

- 'Columbia' and 'Charlotte' sound similar and I have a hearing impairment.

- 'Columbia' and 'Charlotte' look similar so I did not notice the discrepancy at the gate – and neither did the airline staff when checking my ticket.

D.H.

 Solution

Of course, most of the fault lay with the airline not checking properly, but a small part of the blame must be mine for not checking as well. Again, failure to check, rather than simple distraction or any other cause, results in memory failure.

45. International *Forgetting*

In late June 1985, I prepared to move from the USA to Manchester, UK, for the year. Donna and I struggled to get our house ready for a tenant and to pack the things we were taking with us. Simultaneously, I put the finishing touches to a paper that I and a colleague, Roger, were to give in Berlin. I took the paper to the college and made a photocopy to take with me to Berlin. While I was there I also cleared out my office at the college so that it could be used by someone else while I was away. Then Donna, Mandy and I flew together to Kennedy Airport where I saw Donna and Mandy off on a flight to Manchester. A couple of hours later I took a flight to Berlin.

Once on the aircraft I sat back and said to myself: 'At last you deserve to relax.' I went quickly to sleep, well before any of the other passengers, and awoke after a few hours. The cabin was dark and most of the other passengers were sleeping. I felt deliciously relaxed: awake but still half asleep. I decided to use this time to plan what I needed to do once I was in Berlin. While I was imagining getting settled into my lodging and going over the paper I was to present at the conference, I asked myself where the paper was. Instantly my body tensed because I knew immediately that I didn't have the paper with me. In my mind's eye I could see it sitting on my desk at the college, just where I had put it when I was clearing out my office.

Once the shock of this realization wore off, I remembered that I had brought my computer disks with me, to work on once I went to the UK after the conference. One of these disks had the draft of the paper. After hunting all over Berlin, Roger and I found a computer store, where we printed a copy of the paper, which we were able to give at the conference after all.

D.H.

It is at the airport that travel stress probably reaches its climax and the effect on memory can be amazing.

1. Travel Documents

How is it possible, as so many people find, to forget where you have put your tickets, passport and money while simply standing in a line waiting to board an aircraft or while buying a cup of coffee? Often what happens, of course, is that documents are passed between people in conditions of great distraction, and one or the other forgets that this has happened. Thus there is the inevitable argument of: 'I gave it to you', 'No you didn't', 'Yes, I did!'

If you cannot find your travel documents it is essential to be aware of the problems produced by the extra stress and to stay calm, stop blaming other people and retrace your steps. It is common in these situations to put things where you don't normally keep them. We all panic at times, so don't be too hard on yourself.

In one instance, while returning from a recent memory conference, M.G. panicked because all his money and credit cards were not where he usually put them. Instead of remaining calm he panicked, making accusations of his pockets being picked, until he put his hand in another pocket and found the missing items! What his memory expertise has taught M.G. was that, if things are not in one of your pockets, try the other pockets!

2. Boarding

One recurring nightmare of travel is that you will board the wrong aircraft. If you do a lot of flying, you run the danger of becoming too casual and not checking the destination properly. Of course, the airline staff should spot the problem, but

Reasons for Memory Failure

This potentially embarrassing memory failure for a memory expert was completely understandable! Mental overload and distraction caused by a major life upheaval – moving – together with an absence of an adequate self-checking procedure are operating in this failure.

Solution

As noted with previous examples, whenever you have to go somewhere important it is essential to divorce yourself from distractions and go through a checklist of all the important items you need. For important events it is a good idea to write out a checklist and refer to it! For a conference it might be your slides, notes, etc. As has been stressed before, it is very important for you to accept that, although your memory may be very good, it can fail.

they probably think that passengers know where they are supposed to be going! Also there is a tendency among hardened travellers to get engrossed in a book or a newspaper so that they don't realize that all the other passengers have disappeared. If this is a problem for you, the solution is simple: don't read while you are waiting to board an aircraft!

3. Collecting Your Luggage

Apart from the normal stress of wondering whether your luggage will turn up in Brazil, Barbados or the UK, or has even been off-loaded from your aircraft, remembering and identifying your own luggage is becoming a nightmare because so many pieces of luggage look very similar. This means that, after a tiring flight, distinguishing your luggage from the rest (the classic interference problem of memory) becomes a major headache. The obvious solution is to make your luggage distinctive, e.g. by putting large stickers of your home town on the sides.

In the experience of both authors, there is a hard way to learn this! M.G. had a somewhat unusal problem when it came to identifying his luggage. He had a 'soft' suitcase that folded over to allow suits to be carried. The suitcase was green on the outside. However, during the flight, it was folded over the 'wrong way', so that it was brown on the outside. On arriving in Frankfurt, M.G. waited for his green case to appear, but it never did, so he complained to the airline official that his luggage had been lost. The official and M.G. went back to the luggage carousel and observed this single piece of luggage going round and round. When the official took it off the carousel and inspected it, lo and behold, it was M.G.'s luggage with the green cover on the inside. It was not only embarrassing for M.G, he was also late for his appointment!

46. A Forgotten Appointment *for Photographs*

We had an appointment to renew a passport for my son, Zachary, and needed to get passport photographs by a certain date. The photographs had been taken and we were waiting for a phone call telling us to come and pick them up. For some reason the photographer was slow in preparing the prints, so I called her and complained that the photographs had not been done on time and that any further delay might prevent us from catching our flight, for which we had reservations. The photographer was apparently convinced that she had put us in a difficult situation because she then offered to collect the photos from the shop and meet us at 6.30 p.m., an hour and a half after the normal 5 p.m. closing time.

Donna and I discussed who should go to get the photos. Donna already had many things to do, so I volunteered. However, I realized that I had

already agreed to meet Matt, who was helping me fix the speakers on our car. So Donna said she would go after all. We then had an early dinner.

As we were finishing dinner, a friend called to remind us that we had about an hour left to vote on a school bond issue and our vote was important to getting the issue passed. The school bond was important to us, apart from the fact that everyone in our small town knows who does, or does not, vote on crucial issues. We gobbled down what food remained, left the dishes as they were and, since it was a beautiful day, we cycled into town.

At 7.30 p.m. the phone rang. It was the photographer who, in a rage, screamed that we had failed to turn up at 6.30 p.m. when she had come in especially to meet us. There was nothing we could do except apologize.

Reasons for Memory Failure

Some memory failures are possibly best described as a disaster, combined with distraction and a failure of social cueing! Donna claimed that she truly misunderstood the time to pick up the photos. As for me, I did not misunderstand the time so the problem remains of why I did not remember and remind Donna to go when she should have. I believe that I first jettisoned responsibility to remember when Donna agreed to go. The call to vote changed priorities; voting was very high priority. *D.H.*

Solution

Always retain some responsibility for a joint action, even though someone else agrees to carry it out. This responsibility might take the form of reminding the other person if he/she appears distracted or may have forgotten. Of course, you have to be sensible about social cueing (reminding). Reminding your partner constantly about future actions can become irritating if it is overdone. However, where it is done sensitively in situations where forgetting is likely to occur, e.g. where there is a lot of distraction, then reminding is usually welcomed. It is a good idea to have an agreement with your partner about recurring chores and about what each of you expects from the other. Whenever you make an appointment, write it down and place a note where you will both see it.

47. The Tutorial *Time Failure*

For well over 20 years, I have met small groups of students in my office to tutor them and to discuss their work. I always arrange tutorials with the students at a time that is mutually convenient. This is almost always on a day when I will be in my room for most of the time because I have lectures at other times. As far as I can remember, I have never failed to turn up to such tutorials.

Last year, however, in the name of efficiency, the system was changed. Tutorial times were arranged and fixed by the departmental administrator and tutorial rooms were booked elsewhere in the department by the administrator. This year I failed to turn up for three of my tutorials.

Reasons for Memory Failure

Many failures occur when environmental cues no longer support a 'memory fail-safe' situation. Students previously would 'naturally' turn up in my room and would automatically cue me to hold a tutorial. This cue vanished with the new regime under which my classes were arranged. The 'new' tutorials were arranged at many different times during the week and the tutorials were not held frequently.   M.G.

Solution

Remembering to do something is often a matter of arranging the world so that you will be automatically cued to take some action at the correct time, hence the success of reminding devices, such as bleepers. Using a diary would, of course, have solved the problem, although diaries are not foolproof if people do not consult them regularly or forget what they have read soon after using them. In a case where the world changes, using a diary is a lot better than doing nothing. In this particular case of scheduling tutorials, the new system was so unpopular and prone to disaster that the problem was resolved by going back to the old system!

48. Who Forgot *the House Keys?*

On two occasions, my wife and I have gone out together and both of us have forgotten our house keys. On both occasions this has involved the embarrassment of getting friends to use a ladder to climb in through the top-floor window because both of us are afraid of heights!

Reasons for Memory Failure

The failure to check that another individual is responsible for some act of remembering where responsibility is ambiguous is an obvious memory-failure situation waiting to happen. Both of us assumed the other had the key and both forgot to check whether this was the case. It is a matter of diffusion of responsibility. I blame my wife, since she is usually the person in the family who sees to these things. She, of course, blames me for never taking the responsibility of acting as the family social cue.   *M.G.*

Solution

After two or three such failures, the situation becomes self-correcting, since remembering to take a key when both partners go out becomes a very high priority and there is constant social cueing from each partner to remind the other to take a key. Usually both partners end up taking a key! Devices to hide keys can sometimes help, e.g. put a spare key in some spot in the garden which no burglar is likely to find, such as under a stone. It is even possible to buy a device that looks like dog mess, in which you can hide a spare key in case you forget your own! Magnetic boxes for hiding a spare car key, which can be attached to your car, can also be purchased.

49. Chalk *Airlines*

Tony was the cruise director for a cruise line when I was a post-graduate at Rutgers University. Frequently I would fly down to Florida, where we owned an apartment, and then fly to the Bahamas the next day to meet Tony and sail back to Florida with him. This time, I had just dropped off my hire car and was about to board the bus to the terminal when the driver wanted to know which airline I was taking. 'I don't know,' was my truthful answer. I simply could not recall the name 'Chalk'. 'Lady,' the driver said to me, 'You can't get on this bus if you don't know where you're going.'

Reasons for Memory Failure

The name 'Chalk' is unusual for an airline. Unusual names in themselves probably do not cause memory failure, except that they do not so readily come to mind when going through a list of possibles. As noted elsewhere, flying is a stressful experience for many and this too leads to memory failure. The present lapse was a failure to retrieve what was known, i.e. a memory block. *H.N.*

Solution

Experiencing memory blocks is a frequent occurrence. Whether you are trying to remember names of people or things the basic method for dealing with memory blocks is dealt with on p. 88.

50. Forgetting the Map *of Chicago*

While staying with Doug Herrmann in Terre Haute, I needed to visit Chicago, about 200 miles (320 kilometres) away. Doug's wife, Donna, found a couple of maps of Chicago and put them on the table. Twice she reminded me to take the maps but I had got into my car and was backing out of the drive when she came running out of the house to present me with them. Her smile was triumphant! What a memory expert! No better than her husband! Two weeks of discussing memory and I could not remember to take the maps.

Reasons for Memory Failure

While maps are obviously helpful, by and large I have always tended to rely on road signs and asking people if I get lost. I was pretty confident of finding my way to (and my way round) Chicago – it was a straight road! It is therefore likely that, to some extent, I forgot to take the maps because I did not regard them as too important, but I would have taken them if I had remembered. *M.G.*

Solution

The solution to memory failure caused by a lack of motivation is not to think about it as a memory failure! However, when someone reminds you to do something you know is sensible, you should regard it as a useful gift and use it as you would any other useful gift.

Appearing Incompetent

We accept that the distinction between this category and the last one is very arbitrary. However, this section contains many examples where the individual concerned should have been competent enough to prevent a memory failure, but it happened nevertheless.

51. Forgetting the *Punch-line!*

Many years ago, I, together with a colleague, Bob Sykes, agreed to present a lecture on memory to the Psychology Department at Bristol University. All went well until the very last line of my talk – the punch-line – when

I went completely blank and could not remember the whole point of the paper. It goes without saying that I had no notes. I froze for a minute, before having the inspired idea of asking my co-author, Bob Sykes. Unfortunately, this proved to be an equally disastrous move, since he had to admit that he had not been attending and, indeed, had been thinking of other things during the talk. It was one of those days.

Reasons for Memory Failure

This failure had three causes:

- I was over-confident that I could remember without notes.

- The situation was much more stressful than I had anticipated and so I dried up.

- My co-author failed to provide me with assistance when it was needed. *M.G.*

 ### Solution

This problem is one of the easiest to solve. Whenever you give a speech or a talk, no matter how well prepared you are, or what memory system you use to remember points you wish to make (see pp. 87–99), always keep short notes of the main points in your pocket or purse.

52. The Job Application *that Wasn't*

In autumn 1987 I applied for a number of jobs for cognitive psychologists specializing in memory. One of these jobs was at Purdue University, which had one of the best programmes on memory in the USA. I received a letter of receipt for my application materials. This letter very diplomatically noted that I had failed to enclose my résumé, contrary to what my covering letter had indicated, and asked me to please send it on. I was so embarrassed that I never sent the résumé at all.

Reasons for Memory Failure

I forgot to include the résumé because:

- I prepared the package of application materials in stages.

- I did not check the envelope's contents before mailing because of being in a rush, finding the act of checking tedious and trying not to care too much about the job. *D.H.*

 ### Solution

Time and again the problem of memory failure is the problem of not *checking*. So many memory failures would be avoided if time was set aside for checking important actions rather than assuming that everything is all right. Whenever we rush we run the risk of glossing over details which can act as memory cues and so we become more prone to memory failures.

53. Forgetting to *Give a Lecture*

I was sitting in my room at 2.40 p.m. one day, when two of my students knocked at my door and asked me whether I was going to give the memory lecture scheduled for 2.30 p.m.. I rushed down to the lecture theatre and gave my lecture.

Reasons for Memory Failure

I was so engrossed in writing up a paper on memory that I forgot to check the time.   *M.G.*

Solution

The problem illustrated in this example is to some extent self-correcting. It was such a traumatic experience it has never happened again! To some extent memory failures can be a matter of priorities – and giving lectures at the right time is a very high priority for a university lecturer in memory!

54. Leaving My Briefcase *in the Same Place Twice!*

I went to lunch at Crossroads Restaurant with Bob Levy in about March 1996. Over lunch we discussed various aspects of business for the psychology department and for the university. We returned to our offices at Indiana State University. Later that afternoon I received a call from the owner of the restaurant, telling me that I had left my briefcase, made of blue cloth, and that I could pick it up at my convenience. For some reason, the owner knew that I was a specialist in memory and she kidded me about my memory lapse.

In the year that followed, Bob Levy and I lunched at Crossroads about twice a month. In July 1997 we went there once more to have lunch. I sat down and put my blue cloth briefcase by my side. We had a good discussion, enjoyed our lunch and topped it off with a raisin-oatmeal cookie. We paid and left. As we were crossing the street, the owner came running out and shouted to me that I had left my briefcase. She held up two fingers as I came over to retrieve it. It is very tough being a memory expert who has memory lapses but it is especially tough when someone observes you forget in exactly the same way twice!

Reasons for Memory Failure

Of course, if you don't want to remember your work, why take it with you in the first place! I forgot the briefcase because the lunches were enjoyable; social engagements took my mind off my work. Had I carried my big and bulky leather briefcase, it would have been harder to forget it, but the blue cloth one lay flat.

D.H.

 Solution

Forgetting briefcases is another very common phenomenon. It is, of course, more likely to happen when the contents are not of great importance to the individual and when the briefcase vanishes from sight. Keeping the briefcase in your line of vision is one way of solving the problem. Another solution, if you are desperate, is to attach the briefcase to your wrist with a cord. Secret-service agents do this to prevent theft, but it works as a memory aid as well! Keeping your spectacles on a string, so you are permanently attached to them even when they are not in use, is also a really good way of helping you to remember where you left them – i.e. around your neck!

Offending **Others**

Many memory failures that affect other people are clearly not meant to offend and cannot reasonably be taken as offensive. On the other hand, some memory failures *do* seem offensive, whatever the intention of the forgetter. This often happens where the forgetting is interpreted as showing that the person forgotten was not of importance to the forgetter. It is bad news, therefore, to forget a partner's birthday, to forget to turn up for a date, to forget the name of an old friend, etc. Perhaps it is more important to develop ways of avoiding these problems in these particular situations than in others. Who knows, it may save your marriage!

55. The Forgotten *Date*

In the spring of my senior year I was going steady with a terrific girl named Carolyn. Unfortunately, her religion was different from mine and both of us considered this a problem. Also, despite my affection for her, I was not ready to get married. I told Carolyn that, to give our relationship a test, we should date other people. I didn't really want to do this but, because of the religion problem, we both decided that it was sensible.

In the following week I called a girl at a nearby school for a date to the Saturday dance and she accepted. We agreed that I should pick her up at around 8 p.m. after I finished work at the Charcoal Pit.

I saw Carolyn on Thursday night and told her that we would go out Friday night but, in line with our new non-steady agreement, I had a date with someone else for Saturday night.

On Saturday, I worked at the Charcoal Pit until 7 p.m. then went home, showered, put on a sportscoat and drove to the dance. At the dance, I talked with a few of my friends and danced with a few girls. Then a friend said: 'Say, I thought you had a date with Diane Smithy tonight. What happened?' I was stunned. By this time it was 9.30 p.m., well past the time I was due to pick up Diane and far too late to use the 'I was delayed' excuse.

I called Diane and apologized. I told her that I had been delayed because I had lost track of time and asked if I should still come over. She coolly said 'No' and hung up. I tried to call Carolyn to see if she was free to go out but, of course, she had found a date of her own in the meantime. Philosophically I rationalized that I would not have truly enjoyed myself with Diane.

Reasons for Memory Failure

As has been seen in several other memory failures, motivation sometimes plays a part. I did not really want to date someone else and I felt guilty for dating and being disloyal to Carolyn. However, this failure was not just a simple question of not wanting to remember; the thing to be remembered was not a high priority or 'centre stage' in my mind, and so I didn't take any steps to cue my memory.   *D.H.*

Solution

There is almost no solution to this kind of memory failure. If you really don't want to do something, forget it! It would, of course, be better still not to agree to do something like arranging a date in the first place. Whenever you agree to do something that you don't really want to do, there is a real danger of having a memory failure. If you can, try to persuade yourself that you want to do it, whether it is a date or a chore.

56. Forgetting a *Friend's Birthday*

I had not long started my first year at university and was getting used to new lectures, lecturers, living with new people and being away from home, etc. I went home at the end of October and saw my best friend, Mark. I commented on his coat and remarked: 'That's nice – is it new?' He replied: 'Yes, I was given it for my birthday.' At this point I realized that I had forgotten his birthday.

Reasons for Memory Failure

None given.   *Anon.*

Solution

Forgetting the birthday, anniversary, etc. of a loved one or friend is a very common and major problem, since it is always taken as an indication that the offending party no longer cares as much as he/she once did.

One of the embarrassing failures in everyday life is receiving Christmas cards from friends you have forgotten to send cards to, or forgetting birthdays and anniversaries.

1. Birthday Cards, etc.

One way of remembering birthdays and special dates is to use the Digit Letter Memory System (see p. 93). A more general approach is to make a note in a diary of every relative and friend whose birthday, anniversary or special day you want to remember. You then buy cards for every date at the beginning of the year and consult the diary regularly.

2. Christmas Cards

One approach is to make a note at Christmas of all those who send cards to you, so that you can send cards to them the following year. Obviously, you should add any new friends you make during the year.

Of course it is helpful (good memory etiquette) if your partner starts dropping hints about presents, or where you will both go on the birthday, but some partners deliberately do not do this in order to see whether the other will indeed remember! One thing you should not do is take your partner at their word when they say they do not want a present for their birthday – they may be lying, and if you believe them you may be in trouble!

57. Mistaking One Person *for Another*

A woman in another part of the building where I worked, Susan, recognized me and said her own name, noting we had met previously. I could not recall having done so, although I noticed she had a frumpy look, like another woman I knew well, Fran.

About a week later, I had been thinking about this woman so that I would recognize her and remember her name when I encountered her again. I was just returning from a successful meeting, and was in good spirits, when a woman crossed my path from an angle and said: 'Hello Doug.' She looked like Susan, or at least as I recalled her. My initial impression was that it *was* her and I called her 'Susan'. When I was less than three or four steps past her, I realized that the woman I had just passed was Fran. I felt stupid and embarrassed.

Reasons for Memory Failure

Calling people by the wrong name is, of course, embarrassing, as well as being a common memory failure. This situation partly arose from comparing two people who looked similar but were not terribly 'close' to me, the 'forgetter'. Another factor of significance in this case, over-confidence, occurs regularly in memory failures and results in less efficient checking of what you recall. *D.H.*

Solution

If you are not sure about a person's name, do not call them anything.

58. We Forgot *the Dog!*

My wife Donna, my daughter Mandy and I, with our dog Rusty, went to visit Donna's sister and family, the Sheets, who lived in Connecticut. We stayed there for two nights. When we left on Sunday afternoon all the Sheets – Barbara, Roger, Julie and Jill – came out to say goodbye. Farewells in Donna's family can be quite prolonged – involving thanks for the hospitality, thanks for coming, expressing the desire to see each other again, speculating on when we might get together again, whose turn it is to visit each other, etc. We cheerfully loaded up the car, dutifully and cheerfully waved goodbye and started on our 4-hour journey home. We had driven about 45 minutes when we realized that Rusty was not with us. Chagrined, we turned around and went back to pick him up. We got home late that day.

Reasons for Memory Failure

We forgot Rusty because:

- He was out running around and hence there was no cue to put him in the car.
- I lazily depend on Donna to remember.
- The goodbyes occupied my mind to the exclusion of other thoughts, such as 'Where is Rusty?'

Anxiety to get out of a situation – in this case to get going – can lead to a narrowing of what you pay attention to. This probably affected not only me but also my wife, who also had a memory failure. Thus both Donna and I could not remind the other that we had not put Rusty in the car. Of course, Rusty himself was also responsible for this memory failure because he was off somewhere sniffing around, rather than being nearby to remind us to put him in the car! *D.H.*

Solution

As with some earlier examples, whenever you leave to go somewhere else, *check* that you have everything, including the dog! As soon as you leave a building, say to yourself: 'Have I got everything I came with?' It is especially important to do this if you are anxious or upset.

59. The Forgotten *Lunch*

In late December I agreed to meet two good friends, Bill and Harry, for lunch on 14 January at Utiza College. Bill called to confirm this around 5 January. On 14 January, at around 12.20 p.m., Bill called to ask what had become of me. I apologized, feeling terribly embarrassed, and said that 'I had been babysitting and had lost track of time', that I was sorry and asked if I could still come anyhow. Bill said to come along, so I did.

Reasons for Memory Failure

There was a long time gap between being cued (i.e. reminded of the meeting) and the meeting taking place. Because it was vacation time, I felt less constrained to check my schedule. In fact, I was deliberately avoiding my schedule. However, had I realized that I had an appointment with Bill and Harry, I would have taken steps to turn up, such as posting a reminder. Reminding someone on the day of the meeting is a good idea.

D.H.

Solution

When a long gap occurs between making an arrangement and its fulfilment, it is essential to confirm it close to the meeting time. It is a common experience for people to forget, especially if they become involved in other, greater-priority situations. It is memory courtesy to remind people of earlier engagements, including, as noted earlier, phoning up people you have invited for dinner just to check that they are all right. Sometimes things get on top of us so that we need a break. If this happens, always check that there are no appointments you need to cancel.

60. Failing to Recognize *a Colleague*

When I first came to teach at Swansea, there was considerable interaction with the members of staff in our sister university in Cardiff through the activities of the Welsh branch of the British Psychological Society (BPS). I was talking to a colleague in my department one day when we were joined by another person whom I did not recognize. However my Swansea colleague, John, carried out an extended and pleasant conversation with the new arrival and me, until eventually he turned to both of us and asked: 'By the way, do you two know each other?' Simultaneously, I replied '*No!*' and the newcomer replied '*Yes!*' This was, of course, somewhat embarrassing for me and it must have been somewhat deflating for the newcomer.

Then John, in order to overcome the pregnant pause, introduced us. 'This is Dr Jones,' he said confidently. 'Oh, no I'm not,' replied the somewhat bemused newcomer. 'I'm Dr Smith!' Quite clearly Dr Smith must have begun to feel his personal impact was less than it might have been.

In fact, I had met Dr Smith when I applied for a research assistantship in Dundee 2 years previously. There were a number of interviewers on the selection panel, of which Dr. Smith was one. It is hardly surprising, therefore that I did not remember him, but it is somewhat surprising that he remembered me.

Why John attributed the wrong name to Dr Smith also became clearer after discussion. John was a member of the committee of the Welsh branch of the BPS, as was a Dr Jones, who looked remarkably similar to Dr Smith. It was a case of similar appearance causing mistaken identity, but the consequences for Dr Smith's self-esteem must have been unfortunate to say the least.

Reasons for Memory Failure

The first memory failure, i.e. my failure to recognize Dr Smith, is completely understandable, given the changed context of the first and the second meetings. Indeed, it might even be argued that it is counter-productive to carry around a memory of names and faces which are unlikely to be of use at a later time. Painful as it is to fail to recognize someone who recognizes you, it is unreasonable to feel embarrassed, especially as there might be good reasons why this should happen. In this case, my colleague's confusion of two names, the similar physical appearance and the expectation that Dr Jones might be more likely to visit the department since he was on the Committee of the Welsh branch of the BPS all combined to produce the confusion and subsequent memory failure. *M.G.*

Solution

Don't feel guilty or punish yourself about failing to recognize someone whom you have not met for some time, or whom you have only met fleetingly. No one can be expected to remember everyone and think how cluttered your memory would be if you did! Of course, you should not admit to a memory failure unless you have to, since admitting a failure when it is unnecessary can cause pointless hurt on occasion. If you do find yourself failing to remember someone, try clue-gathering (p. 27). It cannot do any harm.

61. My Wife's *Birthday*

For a few years after we were married, I was unsure of the exact date of my wife's birthday. I knew it was either 19 or 20 January but, as the day approached, I became less and less certain which it was. There were, of course, plenty of social reminders that the day was approaching. It took the form of hints on what would make a suitable present, but it did not seem to occur to my wife to remind me of the exact day. I could have phoned her sisters to find out, but that would have given the game away.

One year I thought the problem had gone away when my wife told me I shouldn't buy her anything because we couldn't afford it. What a mistake believing her turned out to be! In fact, she really wanted a present. I usually managed to get the date right but occasionally I got it wrong, with sad consequences until I memorized it.

Reasons for Memory Failure

I forgot my wife's birthday because:

- Birthdays have never been something that I have regarded as being of great significance, so I have never been highly motivated until it became clear that my failure to remember was becoming important.

- I never make a note in a diary of important dates, which I should do, so I have no external cues.

- My wife did not remind me, so basically it was her fault.

- Also, I found the whole business of giving my wife a birthday present fraught because, on a number of occasions, she burst into tears when she felt the present inappropriate. For example, she was not happy when I gave her a record of *West Side Story*, because she had no record-player – and how should I know that lavender water is a present for those of advanced years?!   *M.G.*

Solution

There are simple methods to ensure that you do not forget birthdays, etc. and they certainly work (see p. 93). Now I never forget my wife's birthday, but she is still not usually impressed with what I get for her! On the other hand, my wife has the annoying habit of buying me exactly what I need for my birthday – and she is always right!

Appearing **Rude**

The difference between offending others and being seen to be rude is one of interpreting how deliberate the offence is likely to be and to what extent the forgetter could have done something to avoid it. In the following examples the memory failures were all thought to be deliberate attempts to be rude whereas, in fact, they were not.

62. Forgetting My *Spectacles*

At work, I always exchange Christmas cards with our secretaries. One year Norma, a new, pleasant, but rather quiet secretary joined us and I forgot to get her a card. However, she did not forget to give me one. I therefore rushed out to get her one, forgetting to take my spectacles, without which I cannot read at all. I rushed over to the students' shop and hurriedly bought a card that looked colourful, although the text was a blur and I could not read it. I signed the card, rushed back to the department and presented it to the secretary.

There was a long pause while she read the card, which she then handed to the other two secretaries, who both collapsed in gales of laughter. Because I had forgotten my spectacles and could not read the card, I did not realize that the card was somewhat obscene, depicting a topless woman in a riotous Christmas outfit, and totally inappropriate to a new, quiet, happily married lady! Or anyone else for that matter.

Reasons for Memory Failure

Christmas time is a peak time for memory failures, when all the people to whom you forget to send cards send them to you. You must not be too hard on yourself when this happens. It happens to everyone. There are so many people to remember that some are bound to slip through the net. It is socially courteous to send Christmas cards early so that they act as a cue to remind people to send you a card. If they still don't send you a card, they probably haven't forgotten!

Because of my original embarrassment at having forgotten to give a card in the first place, I rushed to rectify the situation and forgot to ensure I had my spectacles with me. *M.G.*

Solution

There is no real solution to this kind of problem. How could you know that forgetting your spectacles would lead to the selection of an obscene Christmas card? M.G. didn't even know that such things existed!

63. Forgetting to *Wait for a Friend*

My friends and I had arranged to go to a bar on a Friday night and, at the last minute, one of them knocked on my door to say that he was just popping out to get some food. We all agreed to wait for him. However, all the others began to gather and, after finally rounding up everyone, we set off, all in a jovial mood. I only realized we had left this fellow behind when I returned to find a sarcastic note under my door.

Reasons for Memory Failure

'Out of sight, out of mind' is the popular expression. Because my friend had vanished to get food, he was not there to remind me to wait.

Anon.

Solution

Don't expect your friends to wait for you if you go off when they are about to set out to enjoy themselves. This is not a memory failure to worry about! Social interaction demands energy. In other words, it is hard, if enjoyable, work! When we are deep in conversation with someone, it is easy to lose track of obligations and to fail to remember that we should be doing something else. How often, when hosting a party, do we get caught up in an interesting conversation and forget to do our duty as host until our partner reminds us in words of one syllable!

CHAPTER TWO

What Are Memory Failures?

One of the main aims of this book is to demonstrate the importance of memory failures in everyday life. It is quite clear from reading the accounts in Part I that memory failures can have a large number of consequences.

Some memory failures seem funny, at least when viewed from a distance of a few years, although they often they do not seem funny at the time. Indeed, almost all of them are at least an inconvenience – to the forgetter if no one else. Some memory failures have disastrous consequences, such as the woman who reversed her car over her baby. Quite clearly it is very important that we understand much better the causes of memory failure so that we can reduce the number of occasions on which they happen. This is the reason for this book and, in the following chapters, we will discuss the causes of memory failures and what can be done to help reduce their frequency.

It should, however, be said at the outset that there is no single cure for memory failures. Steps can be taken to help in many situations, but luck, e.g. being distracted at critical times, also plays a part. Furthermore, annoying as some kinds of memory failure are, they are often not much more than an annoyance and their importance can sometimes be exaggerated. If you are elderly and cannot remember someone you met at work 30 years ago, so what?

Why Memory Fails

While you have been reading this book, you have no doubt been struck by the variety of the consequences of memory failures and you will almost certainly have been struck by the number of common themes running through them. Perhaps the most striking fact to emerge is that the vast majority of failures had no single cause. Of course, some do have a single cause, such as being distracted at a critical time, but often a whole range of things need to 'go wrong' for a failure to occur.

Memory failures are similar to aircraft or traffic accidents. Typically, these accidents happen because several things go wrong. An example of such a multi-causal failure was the Heathrow car-parking incident (p. 22). M.G. forgot the location of his car because of:

- Memory interference from parking at the same car-park in the recent past.

- Failure to write down the parking place.

- Failure to park the car in the designated section.

- The absence of the physical cues present at the time of parking because it was dark when he went to retrieve the car.

- Being very tired after a long trip and no one else remembering where the car was.

The multi-causal nature of many memory failures is both good news and bad news. The good news is that, because many memory failures have a number of causes, recognizing even one of the causes can reduce future failures. In the example above, the simple expedient of making a much more careful mental note of where the car is parked (using the method outlined in the following chapter) has solved this kind of problem for M.G. Writing down the number is an alternative, but leaves open the possibility of losing the information.

The bad news is that, because there is seldom a single cause of memory failures, there is no single solution to stop them happening. Some memory failures appear to us, in fact, to be unavoidable. This is particularly true if you are distracted by something, or someone, at a critical time. If your baby cries in alarm you will obviously drop everything to attend to the situation and may well forget to carry out other actions you had planned. Sometimes external cues vanish without being noticed, such as the umbrellas which were forgotten because they were placed away from the table and the rain stopped (p. 27)! Sometimes, too, you rely on other people to remind you, e.g. your partner reminds you when it is your mother's birthday or when you need to visit the dentist. When this person has a memory failure, this can, of course, make *you* appear to have a defective memory. While your dentist might well blame you for such a memory failure, it is difficult to argue that you are entirely to blame, any more than if an alarm fails to go off.

Another memory failure that often leaves us feeling embarrassed and guilty is when someone recognizes us but we do not recognize them. This happens to everyone. This failure might mean no more than you met in a situation where *you* were the focus of interest, such as being interviewed for a job, where the other person was just one of a crowd. It may also be the case that some individuals have less memorable faces (or bodies) than you! The point being made is that memory failures sometimes happen without being your 'fault'. It is important, therefore, not to be too hard on yourself, or other people, when a memory failure occurs. Take account of the context of the memory failure before becoming overly critical. As the examples we have given show, many memory failures are complex, involving a number of different causes.

One reason why we should never jump to conclusions about who is to blame for a memory failure is because this can have serious and damaging consequences. For example, it is often unfairly assumed that memory failures are due to the incompetence of the person who forgets. It is also often assumed that the failure to remember someone's name shows a lack of interest in that person, and this can be interpreted as being hurtful or rude. Of course, as a number of examples in the book show, while memory failures can be due to incompetence, they are also due to many other factors, as has been discussed.

To assume that a memory failure is someone's fault may be completely unjust. This goes just as much for the situation in which you fail to recognize or place someone as for forgetting to take some action or other. It follows that, if someone whom you recognize does not recognize you, you should not immediately get upset, but should consider whether, for example, the context in which you are meeting, or the length of time since you last met, might be to blame. In other words, it is often not helpful to react to memory failures by blaming the forgetter for incompetence.

Not all memory failures are blameless. If someone's memory fails repeatedly, and he/she can take reasonable steps to remember, such as using a new alarm clock if an existing one repeatedly fails to work, it is difficult to exonerate him/her.

The examples in the book were experienced by memory experts or people who were mostly very knowledgeable about memory. Nevertheless, the authors do use methods to reduce the incidence of memory failures and, without them, the number of memory failures they suffer would be much greater.

The fact that memory failures happen to memory experts shows the difficulty of everyday memory tasks. Factors such as distraction, anxiety, vanishing cues, meeting people out of context and failures of social reminding are difficult for everyone. Research into what makes these tasks difficult should make it possible to develop procedures for coping with these tasks. Our collection of memory failures reveals that a number of different factors can cause memory failures. Perhaps the three most important are:

- Distraction or preoccupation.
- Cueing failures.
- Failure to process the information to be remembered.

Let us consider these in turn and see what we can learn to prepare us for future memory tasks.

1. Distraction or *Preoccupation*

Many of the memory failures described in this book can, in one way or another, be attributed to an individual being distracted from the memory task on hand. This 'distraction' can have many causes. For example, thinking about a problem which was troubling them has caused both authors, in different incidents, to:

- Drive away from a fuel station without paying (p. 51).

- Drive away from a fuel station with the hose from the fuel pump still stuck in the car (p. 48).

Many alleged shoplifting offences are carried out by individuals who are mentally preoccupied by traumatic events in their recent past, such as a bereavement or marriage break-up. This does not, of course, mean that shoplifting is not a crime nor deny that many people deliberately steal. It does mean that, in some situations, there should be a greater awareness of the reasons for non-payment for goods and a greater realization of the difference between forgetfulness and theft.

In fact, a whole range of factors can cause distraction and preoccupation with events other than the one on which attention should be focused. The 'absent-minded professor' is the classic stereotype of people who have memory failures because they are so preoccupied with their work that they fail to pay attention to the world around them. There are a number of examples in this book where individuals have become so involved in the on-going conversation that they have left their briefcase (p. 67), forgotten the dog (p. 71), etc. Preoccupation and distraction can occur because of enjoyment and excitement as well as depression and anxiety.

It should also be noted that distraction which affects people in one situation may not affect them in another. For example, if you have a well-established habit, then distraction can easily prevent you from altering your normal behaviour and you may inadvertently drive to your place of work instead of the supermarket nearby! On the other hand, if you are trying to follow a completely new route, you are much less likely to be distracted.

One major cause of distraction is arguing with your partner, and this was a factor in the case where someone forgot to put on her panties (p. 24)! But distraction can take so many different forms (moving house, changing your job, having a row with your boss, deadlines at work, parents being distractd by crying babies or playful children) that it is almost impossible to predict.

One major problem with distraction is that it is often beyond the control of the person involved: a child demanding your immediate attention while driving may cause you to have an accident; a phone call giving you important news may cause you to forget to attend a meeting; long-lost friends suddenly turning up on your doorstep may make you completely forget to post an important letter. When distractions come from the outside, when they cause forgetting, and when in that situation most individuals would have had a memory failure, it is important not to blame yourself or others for the memory failure. It is also important to realize that some internal forms of distraction, such as severe pain or severe depression, can also cause memory failure and, again, it is not sensible to blame anyone in these situations.

One problem with distraction is that, even if you are aware of it, there is often little you can do to avoid memory failure. We know of one failure which illustrates this neatly. A mother with young children was distracted by them as she was putting them and an accordion into the car. She placed the accordion on top of the car, sorted out the children and drove off with the accordion still on the roof. At a turning, the accordion shot off the roof and landed on the road in front of the car. Fortunately she was able to stop the car and the accordion was recovered. A week later, just as she was again getting into the car with the accordion, a friend came by who had heard the story of the accordion and stopped to chat about it. While they were chatting, the woman again rested the accordion on the car roof. After telling the story, she got into the car, again leaving the accordion on the car roof. At the identical turning, the accordion again shot off the roof onto the road, but this time a truck ran into it, causing considerable damage which took many months to repair! Clearly experience of the previous distraction did not help in this case!

Of course, as noted above, distraction can come about as a result of preoccupation with on-going problems and here you must be aware of the dangers. You must try to put on-going problems out of your mind in shops or fuel stations and be aware of the dangers. It is no easy thing to do, as the authors' experiences have shown.

2. Cueing *(Prompting) Failures*

One thing that has emerged clearly from the memory failures we have studied is how many times we are 'let down' by the world when it comes to helping us to remember. Remembering often depends on being cued to do things at the correct time, e.g. your partner remembering that you have a dental appointment at 11.00 a.m. or the alarm bell ringing to remind you to get up for an important appointment. We almost certainly don't realize the extent to which our memory is, throughout the day, controlled by external cues, until they fail.

Social Cues

A number of examples illustrate the important of social cueing, i.e. being reminded to attend to a memory problem by your partner, friend or colleague. D.H.'s failure to remember his coat after a meeting (p. 33) was due to the cue vanishing – the coat becoming 'out of sight' – and his host not cueing him by asking, for example, 'Have you got everything?' M.G.'s failure to load the suitcase for a weekend trip was a double social cueing failure, since he did not cue his wife and his wife did not cue him; both assumed the other had attended to the problem (p. 35)!

In many relationships, division of labour occurs so that one partner takes on more responsibility for certain kinds of tasks than others. For example, when going on holiday, one partner might take responsibility for ensuring that the tickets have been checked, the passports are up to date and the invoices are in order, while the other might be responsible for packing the cases. Social cueing often takes the form of asking the partner who has responsibility for, say, packing the suitcases, whether he/she has packed the soap, the suncream, the toilet bag, shoes, shorts, dresses, etc. while the reverse might be true for checking tickets, timetables, etc. If there is a failure of such social cueing, then 'accidents' can happen, such as turning up to the airport a day early in the case of M.G.! (See p. 18.)

One interesting implication of the importance of social cueing for memory failure is that, when someone's partner dies or leaves, the remaining partner is likely to have more memory failures because he/she no longer has anyone to remind them. Clearly relatives need to be aware of this loss of cues and to take care to ensure that elderly parents are socially cued (reminded) of important events.

Physical Cues

Just as important as social cues are physical cues. We use physical cues all the time to remind us about things we should do, such as setting alarm clocks and watches to cue us about the time, which in turn reminds us that, for example, at 2.00 p.m. we must go to a meeting. One of the more interesting problems of remembering, as noted above, occurs when physical cues present at one point in time vanish without our noticing them. A good example of this is the rain stopping. On one occasion, the rain ceasing to fall went unnoticed and therefore failed to cue D.H. that he had left his umbrella behind (p. 27). In another example, a coat 'disappeared' after a door was closed (p. 33).

But just as vanishing physical cues can spell memory failure, many products are being developed that make use of physical cues in new and original ways to stop memory failures. Examples of these are pill boxes which emit a sound to warn the patient that it is time to take a pill and paging devices which remind patients to keep appointments. Some sophisticated cueing devices, such as neuropagers, have been successfully used to help brain-damaged individuals cope much better with everyday living. Interestingly, the fuel pump disaster (p. 48) could not have happened in the UK as the nozzle has to be held in order to fill the tank.

It is also possible for physical cues to stop acting as memory prompts because you just get used to their presence and ignore them. The account of murdering houseplants by forgetting to water them (p. 34) is a common example of this. Because the plants were present all the time in the house their memory-prompting capacity failed. Of course, the plants also died because of a lack of interest (motivation) on the part of the person caring for them.

3. Failures to Process *What You Need to Remember*

Another class of reasons for memory failure is the failure to register in your memory the material to be remembered in the first place. If you do not pay attention to what you are supposed to remember, you obviously will not remember it at a later date. There are a number of reasons why information may not be processed in the first place.

Lack of Motivation

Among the most important reasons is lack of motivation. For example, it might not seem worthwhile to expend any effort on studying material that could well be of no use in the future. A common example of this is paying little attention to the names of people you are introduced to at a party because you do not think you will ever meet again. Obviously, if remembering such a person's name did become 'useful' in the future, this would be too bad. You would fail to remember their name.

However, it is important not to worry too much about this. If we spent our time trying to remember the names of everyone we meet, we would do little else! There are obviously differences between people whom you 'need not' remember and those whom you ought to make an effort to remember, such as your doctor, your teacher or the boss's partner (and boss!). It is reasonable to argue that, if you cannot remember the name of someone you did not particularly want to remember, this can hardly be classed as a memory failure!

Mental Fatigue

Tiredness and depression are two further reasons why good processing might not take place. When you are tired it is difficult to spend the time and energy making sure that you will later be able to recall a fact or an event. Those who are severely depressed also find it difficult to make the effort to process new information properly, again leading to memory failures later on.

Over-confidence

Another major reason why individuals sometimes do not learn material is an over-confidence in their ability to remember, so that they do not spend much effort in learning. An example of this was M.G.'s failure to either make a mental note or write down where he had parked his car at Heathrow airport (p. 22). He was confident that he could remember without effort. His subsequent failure to find his car showed that this was over-confidence rather than confidence. Yet the confidence was to some extent justified because he had never failed to find his car in the past. This example shows how difficult it is to set and maintain a balance between confidence and over-confidence.

Distraction

Distraction can also interfere with your attempts to learn, i.e. when you are trying to make sure you take in information that you want to remember in the future. For example, if you are distracted by someone talking to you when you are visiting a new building, you will not be able to process the new information about the layout of the building and will fail to remember it at a later date. You can, of course, be distracted by internal thoughts as well as external events.

It has to be said that one major reason why we do not process information properly in the first place is related to the way in which our memory systems are built. We have a limited capacity to take in new information and therefore have to make instant judgements about what to pay attention to and what to ignore – and sometimes we make mistakes. However, in some situations, there are methods we can adopt to make it easier to process new information in order to remember it later (see Chapter 3).

* * *

In summary, it is quite clear that memory failures have a variety of different causes and often more than one cause is involved. It is also clear that an individual is often not really to blame for a memory failure if, for example, he/she is distracted at a critical time and so misses important cues, or if the cues vanish without him/her being aware of what is happening.

The three major causes of memory failure are:

- Distraction or mental overload.

- Vanishing social and physical cues.

- Failure to process information properly in the first place, because of lack of motivation or over-confidence.

The next chapter will cover in more detail what can be done to cope with memory failures by looking at:

- Memory systems designed to overcome some of the problems that we all face in remembering.

- A number of different situations where we can do specific things to lessen the chances of certain kinds of memory failure occurring.

But be warned, nothing works all the time!

Part III | Overcoming **Memory Failures**

CHAPTER THREE
Improving **Your Memory**

CHAPTER FOUR
Self-care and **Memory Improvements**

CHAPTER FIVE
The Lessons of **Memory Failure**

Improving **Your Memory**

In the previous chapter we looked at memory failures in general and discussed the three major causes. In this chapter we will describe some specific memory systems and aids which will help you to process and retrieve information and thus avoid memory failures.

Useful **Techniques**

1. Learning New Names and Faces: *Name–Face Association*

One common problem at social events is remembering the names of new people you meet. Forgetting names can prevent potential friendships developing because the person whose name has been forgotten assumes that he/she cannot have been very important. The reverse is also true. Remembering someone's name implies that he/she is important to you or has made an impression on you. Sales-people are well aware of the importance of remembering the names of their clients and there is a simple technique that has been shown in a number of scientific studies to aid name–face association.

All you do is picture a prominent feature of the newly met individual together with his/her name. For example, suppose the new person is called Mr Holly; you might picture him with holly growing out of his nose, if his nose is his most prominent feature. In a similar fashion, you might imagine a Mrs Green with green paint over her chin, if her chin is the most prominent feature.

Of course, there are a number of difficulties to be overcome if you are going to use this method:

1. Not everyone has a prominent feature. This does not really matter because you can *imagine* them with a prominent feature. For example, if someone is called Mr Fox, you can imagine him with a long, 'fox-like' nose.

2. Many people do not have 'easy-to-picture' names. For example, it is not easy to picture a Mr Sykes, Mrs Patel, Mrs Kaminski, etc. In these cases, you should use substitute names, perhaps SOCKS for SYKES, PETAL for PATEL and COME AND SKI for KAMINSKI. Picture Mr Sykes with a sock over his head, Mrs Patel's hair covered in rose PETALS and perhaps asking Mrs Kaminski to COME AND SKI.

3. Some people have common names, such as Smith or Davies. In these cases you will probably be familiar with someone of the same name – perhaps a sporting celebrity. Imagine the celebrity talking to the person who is being introduced to you.

There is no doubt that this method works. It has been shown to help students, learning-disadvantaged individuals and the elderly. The question is not so much 'Does this method work?' but 'How should I use it?'

There are some important rules you should stick to:

1. Don't try to use the method at normal social gatherings, such as parties, in order to remember the name of everyone you meet. Most people find it impossible to create an image and have a sensible conversation at the same time so you run the risk of remembering everyone's name but being thought a complete social idiot!

2. Remember only the names of people you are likely to meet again.

3. When you do meet someone whose name you want to remember, excuse yourself from the situation – perhaps to go to the toilet or get a drink – and then make the visual association.

4. If you don't catch the person's name the first time, ask them to repeat their name. This is not embarrassing because it shows that you are interested in the person.

5. You should think of the person's name from time to time and picture them in your mind's eye in order to refresh your memory.

2. Remembering *Names and Faces*

As discussed previously, one of the most embarrassing experiences that happens to all of us at one time or another is to forget the name of someone who expects us to remember them. (Even so, it is quite rare to fail to recognize your mother – as happened to M.G.!) Often this occurs when you meet someone in an unexpected context, or at a party when you are talking to two people whom *you* know but who obviously don't know each other. You then find yourself unable to introduce them to each other because you have forgotten the name of one of them.

Whatever the situation, you can adopt all or any of a number of strategies:

1. Keep talking in the hope that the conversation will give you a clue to the person's identity.

2. Try to remember the context in which you last met the person.

3. Go through the alphabet to see if this triggers the name. Does it begin with an A, B or so on?

4. If this doesn't work, just keep talking. It is usually better to be thought rude than to admit that you cannot remember the name of your boss, mother, etc.

5. Memory courtesy requires that, when talking to someone you don't know, you should introduce yourself. This prevents the host being embarrassed.

6. Avoid peering at name badges at conferences. This is a dead giveaway. Put pressure on conference organizers to provide name badges in very large print.

7. If you are getting on in years, it is permissible to admit you cannot remember someone's name – although it is a feeble excuse!

3. Learning Foreign Language Vocabulary:
The Linkword Method

One of the major problems of learning foreign languages, as many people find, is that remembering foreign words is both boring and difficult. A recent study of British schoolchildren found that, after 4 years of study, the average child could only correctly identify 800–900 words and that 25 per cent of children appeared to have learned next to nothing!

However, there is a method of learning foreign language vocabulary which has been around for at least 100 years and which has been shown in a large number of scientific investigations to increase learners' ability by a factor of 2 or 3 times. It works like this. You link an English word to another English word that sounds like the foreign word to be remembered. For example:

> *The Turkish for **BLOOD** is **KAN***
> *Imagine pouring out a **CAN** of **BLOOD***
>
> *The Spanish for **RICE** is **ARROZ***
> *Imagine **ARROWS** landing in your bowl of **RICE***

You must spend 10 seconds thinking about each picture or it will not stick in your mind properly. Now study the examples given in the panel overleaf and then test yourself by answering the questions which follow:

Think of Each of These Images in Your Mind's Eye for about 10 Seconds

The Japanese for SHORTS is HAN ZUBON
Imagine my HANDS UPON your SHORTS

The Russian for EYE is GLAZ
Imagine you have a GLASS EYE

The Polish for JUICE is SOK
Imagine drinking JUICE through a SOCK

The Hebrew for ELEPHANT is PEEL
Imagine an ELEPHANT eating orange PEEL

The Polish for HERRING is SLEDZ
Imagine a HERRING sitting on a SLEDGE

The German for BRIDE is BRAUT
Imagine a Belgian BRIDE, a Brussels BRAUT

The Italian for NIGHT is NOTTE
Imagine spending a NAUGHTY NIGHT out

The Portuguese for BUCKET is BALDE
Imagine a BALDY-headed man with his baldy head in a BUCKET

The Spanish for COW is VACA
Imagine a COW with a VACUUM cleaner, cleaning a field

The Turkish for DAUGHTER is KIZ
Imagine I'd love to KISS your beautiful DAUGHTER

© Linkword Programme: Interaktive plc; with permission

What is the English for:

KIZ? ....

VACA? ....

BALDE? ....

NOTTE? ....

BRAUT? ....

SLEDZ? ....

PEEL? ....

SOK? ....

GLAZ? ....

HAN ZUBON? ....

As you can see, this method works for almost any language. Indeed, using this method, one of the present authors has devised courses in 12 different languages which teach not only an extended vocabulary but also basic grammar points, such as genders, pronouns, tenses, word order, etc. A number of studies have shown that 150–200 words and a basic grammar can be learned in a single day using these courses. Compare this with the 800–900 words learned in 4 years at school.

4. Mental Filing: *The Peg Word Memory System*

How many times have you lain in bed at night and come up with a great idea, only to forget it when you wake up in the morning? It happens to everyone, but there is a simple mental filing system which can make this problem a thing of the past.

First you must learn these rhymes. They will enable you to use the *peg-word memory system.*

> 1 is BUN
>
> 2 is SHOE
>
> 3 is TREE
>
> 4 is DOOR
>
> 5 is HIVE
>
> 6 is STICKS
>
> 7 is HEAVEN
>
> 8 is GATE
>
> 9 is WINE
>
> 10 is HEN

Go through these rhymes until you are sure you know them by heart.

To remember objects, ideas, etc. using these rhymes, take the following simple steps. Suppose the first three objects you want to remember on your shopping list are:

> 1. FLOWERS
>
> 2. BANANAS
>
> 3. BREAD

Now picture the first object – FLOWERS – interacting with the first word in the poem – BUN. You might imagine FLOWERS growing out of a large BUN. You then picture the second object – BANANAS – interacting with a pair of SHOES, perhaps a BANANA growing out of a SHOE. Now picture the third object – BREAD – interacting with a TREE, perhaps loaves of BREAD hanging from a TREE.

Try this for yourself by memorizing the following wordlist:

1. DUCK (BUN)

2. ALLIGATOR (SHOE)

3. ARROW (TREE)

4. PENGUIN (DOOR)

5. WATER (HIVE)

6. RIVER (STICKS)

7. TRAIN (HEAVEN)

8. FISH (GATE)

9. PLATE (WINE)

10. BOOK (HEN)

Once you have pictured each of these new words interacting with the peg words, try to recall them in the following order. What word was: third, fifth, eighth, tenth, second, first, fourth, ninth, sixth and seventh?

Most people get six or more words correct and the really amazing thing is that it is possible to tell whether the word you were given was the first or the eighth word, etc.

Of course, just remembering lists of objects is not very useful, but you can use this system to remember ideas you have during the night or while you are travelling to a meeting, when you cannot write them down.

Suppose you have the following ideas:

1. I have to visit **New York**.

2. I have to get money out of the **bank**.

3. I must remember to talk about **prisons** in my essay.

In order to remember these ideas, you could imagine:

> 1. NEW YORK being rained on by BUNS.
>
> 2. Putting your best pair of SHOES into your BANK.
>
> 3. Making a PRISON from TREES.

The method can be used over and over again for new material. You can use it to remember a shopping list if you do not want to write one out, and to remember jokes, as well as using it as a mental filing system. You can also use it for remembering points you wish to make in a speech but, if you do, always make a note of the main points on a piece of paper – just in case!

5. Remembering Strings of Numbers:

The Digit Letter Memory System

Everyone knows that remembering strings of numbers is difficult. This is because numbers are pretty meaningless. Unfortunately, they are often very important, e.g. your partner's birthday, your friend's telephone number, your bank personal identification number (PIN). The system that helps with remembering number sequences is the *Digit Letter Memory System*.

The basic principle involves converting meaningless digits into meaningful words. To use the method, you first have to learn the following:

> 1 = t (there is **one** downstroke in the letter t)
>
> 2 = n (there are **two** downstrokes in the letter n)
>
> 3 = m (there are **three** downstrokes in the letter m)
>
> 4 = r (r is the last letter of the word **four**)
>
> 5 = l (l is the Roman abbreviation for **fifty**)
>
> 6 = sh ('sh' sounds like the s sound in **six**)
>
> 7 = k (the letter k has the number **seven** embedded in it)
>
> 8 = f (the letter f has two loops like the number **eight**)
>
> 9 = p (the letter p is **nine** – 9 – the wrong way round)
>
> 0 = s (**zero** – 0 – starts with an s sound)

You should learn these off by heart before continuing.

The method can be used to remember numbers in the following way:

1. Translate each number into its equivalent letter, e.g. 14 should be TR.

2.. Use any vowel(s) you like to make up a word in which T and R are the consonants, e.g. **TEAR, TOWER, TIRE, TOUR**.

3. Make up a phrase including this word. Suppose you want to remember that your partner's birthday is on the 14th. You might picture her with a **TEAR** in her **EYE** because you forgot her birthday last year!

As another example, suppose your PIN is 5 8 1 0. This gives the letters L F T S, which could be **LOFTS**. You might imagine cash machines in LOFTS. Sometimes it is difficult to think of one word for a PIN. No problem! Split it into two words. For example, 3 0 1 2 gives M S T N, which might be **MY STONE**.

Telephone numbers can be remembered in the same way, although it often takes time to get a good word, or words, for long strings of numbers, so do not try to use this method unless you know you will need to remember the number. As with the memory methods discussed earlier, scientific studies have shown that the Digit Letter Memory System works.

6. Remembering *Car Registration Numbers*

Remembering car numbers often involves remembering sequences of letters and numbers. There are two situations in which you are most likely to want to remember a car number:

1. When you buy a new car or hire a car.

2. If you witness a road accident.

In the UK the number often involves sequences such as K392 FNL. The first letter is usually easy to remember because it indicates the year the car was registered. To remember the number sequence 392, you can use the digit-letter memory system:

3=M

9=P

2=N

You then make up a nonsense phrase, such as **MY PIN**. For the sequence FNL you could make up the word **F I N A L**. So the final letters are **MY PIN FINAL**. When you are trying to remember the number of a car which is, for example, leaving the scene of an accident, the letters are more important than the digits. If you cannot think of a word like FINAL you can make up a phrase such as: FOUL NASTY LOUDMOUTH.

In the USA, a car number might be WMU 131. WMU could be remembered as **WET MEN UNDRESS**. 131 is TMT, which could be TOMATO!

7. Remembering Speeches: *Method of Loci*

The use of memory systems to remember speeches goes back to the Greeks and Romans. Roman orators in particular had to recall very long speeches from memory and resorted to the *method of loci* memory system invented by the Greek orator Simonides.

The method involves using visual pictures to link ideas together. For example, if you want to link the words DOG and BOOK, you could picture a dog eating a book. In using the method of loci, you picture a sequence of places with which you are familiar, e.g. in your bedroom.

1. Starting with your bed, go round the room clockwise, picking out 10 places in your room. For example, next to your bed might be a table, next to the table a chair, next to the chair a dressing table, next to the dressing table a window, etc.

2. Once you have picked out 10 places, go over them again until you are sure you will remember them every time you think about your room.

3. To remember 10 objects, mentally place the first object on the first place (your bed), the second object on the second place (the table), and so on, until all objects have been placed in a location. When you now go through the places in your room mentally, you will be able to recall the objects you have placed in your room.

Try it with this list of objects:

1. TRUMPET	6. HAMMER
2. BOTTLE	7. GUN
3. EGG	8. SPECTACLES
4. CROCODILE	9. SEAGULL
5. TRUCK	10. DIAMOND

To remember points you wish to make in speeches, use the locations of your room in the same way. Suppose the points you wish to make in your speech are:

1. Thank the bride's parents.

2. Toast the bride and groom.

3. Tell a joke about the groom's car, etc.

You might:

1. Picture the bride's parents in **your bed**.

2. Imagine the bride and groom on **your table** next to your bed.

3. Imagine the groom's car crashing through **your window**.

Of course, not all speeches involve points which at first sight are easy to picture. You must turn such points into something which *is* easy to picture. Suppose, for example, you wish to talk about:

1. The **evils** of dictatorship.

2. The value of **democracy**.

3. The need for a **social conscience**.

You might picture:

1. EVIL as Adolph Hitler.

2. DEMOCRACY as the American President.

3. SOCIAL CONSCIENCE as a priest or rabbi.

If you have more than 10 points to make in your speech, you can simply extend the number of locations by thinking of other places that you are familiar with, such as the teeing-off places at your local golf club. One word of warning though. No system of remembering is foolproof. It is highly advisable to write the key points down on a piece of paper – just in case!

8. Improving Spelling: *The 'Story' Method*

One of the problems in spelling generally is that English is often very inconsistent, making it difficult to 'work out' what the correct spelling should be. But there are simple ways of making this easier for yourself or your child. One of the best ways is to make up a 'story' to indicate how the word should be spelled. It is a very good idea to get your child involved in making up the story as this can make spelling fun as well as useful.

Here are some examples:

ACROSS: To remember whether this word is spelt with one C or two Cs, think of the following story: There is only **ONE SEA** (C) ACROSS to America.

SUCCESS: To remember whether this word is spelt with one C or two Cs, think of the following story: You need two eyes **TO SEE** (2C)! SUCCESSFULLY.

CAREFULLY: To remember whether this word is spelt with one L or two Ls, imagine: You will go **TO HELL** (2L) if you do not drive CAREFULLY. (Note also that words like SUCCESSFULLY also have 2 Ls.)

SEPARATE: To remember whether this word has an E or an A after the letter P, imagine: You SEPARATE **A RAT**.

CALENDAR: To remember whether this word ends in ER or AR, imagine that: We make up CALENDARS from the ST**ARS**.

Our advice for helping a child who is poor at spelling is to find as many words as possible which present spelling problems, then make up three or four stories each day. Make sure you and your child can spell each word correctly with the help of these stories. At the beginning of the next day, go over the words already learned to make sure they are correctly remembered, then go onto the next three to four words. Do not work on too many words at one time; three or four each night is enough.

9. Exams and Memory: *The First Letter Memory Aid*

One of the most commonly used memory aids in exams is the *first-letter memory aid*. This involves learning the first letters of points you wish to make in exams. One well-known example of the first-letter memory aid is the phrase 'Richard Of York Gave Battle In Vain' to remember the colours of the rainbow: Red, Orange, Yellow, Green, Blue, Indigo, Violet. Sometimes the letters can be used to make up a nonsense word, e.g. **ROYGBIV**, and this works just as well.

Likewise, the first letters of the words in a phrase can be used to tell you the first letters of the points you wish to remember in exams. Even university students studying for high-level exams often use this method and medical students are notorious for thinking of rude phrases to remember their anatomy notes. However, these phrases are suitable for helping students at school as well as at university and a large number of studies show they are very effective not only for remembering the points students wish to make but also for the order in which the points come.

The first-letter memory aid has also been shown to be effective in helping people to overcome memory blocks, i.e. when you know that you know something but cannot recall it – the 'tip-of-the-tongue' state. One study found that, when people were unable to retrieve a known word, giving them the first letter resulted in them recalling that word over 50 per cent of the time. During exams, when stress is high, people frequently suffer from memory blocks – and this is just the situation that the first-letter memory aid is likely to prevent.

The first-letter memory aid is also likely to be useful in exams for another reason. In order to use the method, you have to organize your ideas long before the exam. You have to think about the topic you are studying and then about the main points you wish to remember so that you can take the first letters of these points and make them into a silly sentence or phrase. The very act of having to think about and organize what you are studying is likely to have major benefits, apart from the extra advantage of being better able to remember the points you wish to make. Once you remember a particular point, then you will remember the things you want to say about that point. In preparing for an exam on great cities, for example, where you may want to talk about New York, London, Paris, Tokyo, Madrid and Berlin, you might use the phrase 'Never Let Praise Turn My Brain'. Once you know which cities you want to talk about, you can picture features of each city and, if you have been studying them, you will know what is special about each.

In order to use the first-letter memory aid in studying for exams, you should go through the following steps:

1. Read through all the relevant material for a topic, making notes as you go.

2. Once you have read as much as necessary, go through your notes to make sure you understand them all.

3. Think about the topic and which points you want to get across.

4. Make notes about how you are going to answer a question on that topic and which main points you will need to recall in order to remember all the other things you want to say.

5. About 2 weeks before the exam, make a note of the main points. Make up a phrase or nonsense word based on the first letters of these main points. But a word of warning! Make sure you prepare an answer that is broad enough to cover a range of questions on that topic.

6. Sometimes you will have too many points for one answer to make only one phrase or nonsense word. If this happens split the points into two and make up two phrases or words.

7. Make sure that you learn the phrases well, so that they come back to you and you can remember what each letter stands for.

8. The evening before the exam, go through all the first-letter phrases to make sure you can remember them and what they stand for. Make sure you are word perfect on this.

9. On the day of the exam, get to the exam room at least half an hour before the exam starts. Do not talk to anyone; just go over your memory aids again and again, making sure you remember them all.

10. When you get into the exam room, look at the questions, then immediately write down all the phrases and the points they stand for which are relevant to the questions you have been asked. That way you can get on with the exam knowing you will not forget the important points you want to make.

Of course this approach does not work for everyone. Nothing works for everyone – even aspirins! What you should do is see whether it works for you. If you find that it takes you forever to make up a useful memory phrase then do not use this method! But it does work for many people. Some people don't use it, not because they find it doesn't work for them, but because they feel it is silly to use such devices or because their teacher thinks it is not the right way to go about studying.

The point is this: however much you know and understand your work, when you are under pressure from exams and the huge quantity of material you need to remember, anyone can forget points they wish to make in exams. Which is sillier: to use 'silly' memory aids that help you remember what you want to say, or to forget what you know because you were afraid to use memory aids in case of what your teachers might say if they found out? Remember, too, that unless the memory aids you prepare are of high quality, you will not be able to write a good answer in an exam. Memory aids help you to reach your potential in exams – they cannot do more.

Using first letters can be used in another way in exams, or in any situation where you have a memory block. When a memory block happens, just go through the alphabet thinking about whether the missing word started with A, B, C, etc. There is evidence that this method will overcome about 25 per cent of memory blocks.

CHAPTER FOUR

Self-care and Memory Improvement

By now, it should be clear that your ability to learn and remember are not the only factors that produce memory failure. In addition, you may fail at a memory task because of your physical, emotional and motivational states, as well as because your particular approach does not suit the memory task.

All your psychological and physiological states acting together can affect memory. Therefore, for your memory to work well, it is important that you know how to take care of your psychological and physiological states.

Self-care and the Human Memory System

Memory is, of course, located in the brain. As you probably know, the brain, including memory, is affected by the physical environment, health, chemicals, emotions, attitudes, motivations, social interactions and the use of physical aids. This chapter explains what you need to know about self-care in order to control your memory better and avoid memory failure.

So far, the solutions to memory failures recommended in this book have emphasized the mental control of incoming information. For example, remaining aware of external cues, such as paying attention to a clock, is a matter of information control. In this chapter we pay special attention to improving memory by controlling the world around us (i.e. by information control) and by self-care.

1. Information *Control*

The control of information refers to controlling the cues that naturally occur to you mentally, in your environment and in your social relationships with others.

Physical Environment

The arrangement of your surroundings has an impact on memory. Objects, signs and visual patterns can often activate memories far more easily than related ideas or thoughts. This is also true for sounds and smells. A large number of commercial products are produced and sold explicitly as memory aids. For example, a tape-recorder allows us to avoid memory failure by enabling us to hear again what someone has already said. Similarly, photographs keep us from forgetting what others look like because they remind us how they looked on a certain occasion. Alarm devices remind us far better than we can remind ourselves. If you take care to use such devices when it is important, you will remember.

Most alarm devices are designed to help memory in specific situations. For example, everyone has at some time left their car in the large parking area of some gigantic shopping mall, only to have difficulty finding it later on. Now you can buy a remote transmitter that, at the press of a button, will make your car's lights blink and its horn sound. Another recent device is a specially designed wallet that sets off an alarm if you try to close it without replacing your credit card.

In the past few decades, computerized products have been developed that help people with memory problems. Some of these products have been called 'teaching machines' because they are used to train a person's memory ability. Computerized courses and, most recently, interactive computerized courses can train your memory skills as never before. An important feature of the computerized approach is that memory-training programmes can teach people memory skills using simulations of the everyday situations in which the skills are used.

Social Environment

You are more likely to have a memory failure when you are with others than when you are alone. Social pressure makes it stressful to hold dissenting views among friends or acquaintances. People who recall something differently from others can face an enormous amount of scepticism about the accuracy of what they recall and are sometimes convinced that their memory was wrong when in fact it was right. Taking care of your relationships with others will also enhance your memory in social contexts.

Another source of error comes from the pacts we make with other people. We agree to share the burdens of learning and remembering tasks: 'You remember to pick up the kids and I will remember to pick up the groceries.' Pacts are especially common between people who live together because home-life requires the dividing up of chores. Pacts are also common between co-workers, who may similarly divide work responsibilities. Unfortunately, we sometimes fail to pay attention to the pact we have made and then fail to remember what was expected of us.

The flow of conversation is yet another factor interfering with our memory. If information goes by too quickly, many of us fail to retain what was said. If a speaker talks too softly, we may have difficulty grasping everything. Unfortunately, we may be expected to recall the conversation later.

2. *Strength*

Strength limits how much energy you can devote at any one time to doing anything, including a memory task. This strength derives from your physical condition, health and use of chemicals (ranging from beverages to medicines).

Physical State

Memory requires energy. If you are tired then your memory will not perform as well as usual. If you want to depend on your memory, you must make sure that you are getting the right things to eat and enough sleep, rest and exercise. Your strength and your ability to do memory tasks go in cycles throughout the day and your attentiveness varies with changes in your strength. Therefore your memory functions best at certain times of the day. Most people find that it peaks somewhere around mid to late morning and in the middle of the afternoon.

Sleep Your sleep pattern also affects when you are physically most fit for memory tasks. If you go to bed early and get up early, you will probably learn more readily at the beginning of the day. If you go to bed late and get up late, you will be sharper later in the day. If you work a nightshift or during weekends, your peak times will be different from those of people who work weekdays from nine to five. Identify your peak times and try as far as possible to perform memory tasks when you are most alert.

Memory suffers with changes in your daily or weekly cycle. Such changes require an effort to readjust, reducing your memory performance. A particularly strenuous change occurs when you have to travel across time zones. After crossing several time zones, people get 'jet lag' and can find it hard to remember the directions to their hotel or, once in the hotel, to remember the number of their room.

The amount of sleep you get is important to effective memory performance. A good night's sleep will make you alert for memory tasks. A late night spent studying or at work will result in fatigue that can interfere with learning and remembering the next day.

Diet How much you eat affects your memory. If you eat too little, you will become malnourished and more prone to memory and other errors. If you eat too much, you will become mentally sluggish and perform memory tasks poorly. What you eat also affects your memory. Many nutritionists have proposed that vitamins help memory, but there is considerable debate about which vitamins are most important. Nutritionists generally advise that a normal, healthy diet supplies enough vitamins to guard against memory-related deficiencies. Generally, protein-rich foods – beef, pork, kidneys, liver, fish, shellfish, milk, eggs, cheese – are believed to facilitate memory.

Exercise A lack of exercise can increase memory failure. On the other hand, memory is improved if you are physically fit. Exercise improves your cardiovascular condition, reduces stress and depression, and improves digestion and sleep – all of which help memory.

Health

Physical Impairment Poor eyesight or poor hearing often interferes with registering information in the memory or retrieving it from the memory. If you cannot hear or see something clearly, you cannot be expected to learn or remember it clearly. If you think that one of your senses is impaired, get yourself examined by a physician. You may discover that all you really need is a loudness booster for your telephone or a magnifying glass for reading fine print. If you need spectacles or a hearing aid, you will be glad when you get them and you will perform far better at the memory tasks that others ask of you.

Many people think that memory failures occur only because their brain is not working well. Unfortunately, we often cannot remember something because we are unable to see or hear it in the first place. If we do not register information, it is obvious that we will be unable to remember such information later.

Illness When we are ill we have significantly more memory problems than when we are in good health. For example, a bad cold interferes with learning and remembering, and influenza or an upset stomach will have essentially the same effect. Illnesses associated with pregnancy, such as high blood pressure, have been known to produce temporary memory problems.

Some illnesses are well known for interfering with memory and these are often called 'memory illnesses'. Alzheimer's disease is the most widely known, while Korsakoff's syndrome, often caused by excessive alcohol consumption over a prolonged period, involves a severe loss of the ability to register new memories. A major stroke will send a blood clot to the brain and disrupt memory, sometimes permanently. Mini-strokes send many tiny clots to the brain and also impair memory. Very low blood pressure, a life-threatening condition, reduces ability to pay attention and learn. Severe depression impairs memory, although this is not permanent. Recent medical research has led to new treatments for all of these memory diseases and they result in minor or even substantial improvements in memory. In most cases it is critical to get medical help as soon as possible in order to get the maximum benefit from treatment.

Chemical State

Medicines and Stimulants We often think that medicines are good for us. However, many kinds of medicine interfere with memory performance. The chemical constituents of medicines used for colds, influenza or allergies, whether they are obtained with or without a prescription, can make us drowsy and impair memory performance. Medicines that affect mood, e.g. tranquillizers and antidepressants, also impair memory.

Any medicine that makes you feel nervy, e.g. stimulants and many diet pills, and even some antibiotics, have been found to impair memory. Coffee, tea, fizzy drinks and tobacco are stimulants that have no effect on memory in small amounts but can make us jittery and interfere with memory when taken in too large an amount. Prescription stimulants are also a poor way to arouse yourself for a memory task. If you are tired they may keep you awake, but too much of a stimulant will make you more easily distracted and more prone to memory error. What helps memory the most is a dose of motivation.

Alcohol and Drugs Alcohol is sometimes called 'amnesia food' because it can erase people's memory of occasions when they have been drinking excessively. In addition, excessive use of alcohol over years destroys tissue in the brain's stem and cortex, reducing learning ability. Excessive alcohol use leads to a loss of accumulated knowledge about how to do things and past experiences. Such losses invariably lead to memory failures. Marijuana and other mind-altering drugs likewise impair memory performance immediately after use and possibly indefinitely.

3. Developing Your Inclination *for Memory Tasks*

If you do not want to perform a memory task, then you cannot fail at it. However, others may claim that you do not want to perform a memory task because you fear that you will fail at it. Our inclination to perform a memory task depends on our attitude, emotional state and motivation.

Attitude

We have different attitudes to all kinds of things and these affect how our memory functions.

Positive and Negative Attitudes Believing that your memory ability is poor or terrible overall will make a memory failure more likely because, if you think you are going to fail anyway, you won't try so hard to remember. If you dislike doing a memory task, this negative attitude may also lead to memory failure. However, an unrealistically positive attitude about your memory will also cause your memory to fail. Where, for example, you think your memory is so good that you do not take any extra steps to remember, you may fail – as M.G. did when it came to remembering where he had parked his car at Heathrow airport (p. 22). The most useful attitude to your memory is to be realistic.

Other People's Attitudes The attitudes of others can influence our attitudes about ourselves. For example, the authors, although you may not realize it, have a reputation for memory performance and our reputation can affect our confidence in performing memory tasks in any circle of acquaintances or co-workers.

Memory Stereotypes There is a variety of stereotypes about memory that have to do with age, sex, race and other characteristics. For example, many older people believe that memory loss is inevitable with increasing age. Unfortunately, older people who believe their memory is poor because of their age are more likely to suffer memory failure than people of the same age who do not believe their memory has been seriously eroded. It is sad but research indicates that people are still affected by stereotypes, even when they claim not to be. The fact is that memory stereotypes are generally inaccurate. Many people do not get significantly worse at memory tasks as they age. Young people do perform better at new and novel tasks but, when it comes to learning and remembering new information in a particular field, they are at a disadvantage compared with an older person who is experienced in that field.

Emotional State

Your emotional state has an important impact on memory performance. If you are in a cheerful, positive state of mind, you will learn and remember more easily than if you are feeling depressed and negative. A poor emotional state interferes with your ability to focus attention.

Stress This especially produces memory failure. High-stress jobs lead to more memory failures than low-stress jobs. Too much anxiety before a memory task will distract you and hamper your recall. For example, when under a great deal of stress, parents forget to pick up their children from school or otherwise loyal employees fail to do critical projects for their boss. A little anxiety will keep you alert and ready to tackle memory tasks as they arise. An intermediate amount of pressure will make it least likely that your memory will fail. If your memory is not working as well as usual, take steps to reduce the stress in your life.

Motivation

Rewards and punishment affect memory in ways that we would expect. We register information in our memory when we have a strong desire to do so. Negative motivation reduces our ability to pay attention. When you have trouble learning or remembering, check your motivation. If you have little incentive to remember something, try rewarding yourself.

4. *Potential*

We all have potential but what we have potential *for* varies from person to person. If we have a potential that is relevant to a memory task, we should do well at it. If we do not have that potential, then we will need to work harder at the task. The three factors relevant to our potential to perform memory tasks are discussed overleaf:

Expertise

Experiences in our job backgrounds equip us with specific skills for the memory tasks we experience on the job. For example, an accountant becomes especially able to recall numbers. Expertise gleaned from hobbies also makes us better at remembering information about our hobbies.

Memory Competence

People differ in how well they perform memory tasks. Knowing what kinds of memory tasks we do well at influences our desire to attempt these tasks. With increasing age, we may lose confidence in our memory competence and this may interfere with our willingness to perform memory tasks.

Personal Style

Some people are especially careful at everything they do, including memory tasks. Other people are careless. A habit of being careful or careless obviously affects how much that person will experience memory failures. Some people are oriented more toward their thoughts than to what is going on around them. Others are aware of everything that is happening but do not think much about their own life. People who are thought-oriented will miss cues and forget to perform memory tasks relevant to these cues. On the other hand, people who are aware of the cues around them may forget their intention to perform certain memory tasks which are not cued by the environment.

Assessing Your Readiness for Memory Tasks

In order to keep your memory sharp, you need to keep track of all these different memory modes for a few days. The checklist opposite summarizes what you need to check before performing important memory tasks. To ensure that your memory performs successfully, you need to anticipate when certain modes might cause trouble. You cannot take steps to improve any particular memory mode unless you have first evaluated all of them. Use the checklist to evaluate your memory modes before you face those situations, such as exams, where you want to ensure successful memory performance.

Memory Readiness Checklist

1. Information

- **Mental Procedures** Are you using your thought processes to encourage memory.

- **Physical Environment** Are you using your physical environment to improve your memory.

- **Social Environment** Are you interacting with others in ways that encourage memory, e.g. memory pacts.

2. Strength

- **Physical State** Does your daily life tire you?

- **Health** To what extent are you free of physical or emotional disorders or debilitating conditions?

- **Chemical State** Are you using substances or medicines which may alter your neurochemistry or other physiological states?

3. Inclination

- **Attitude** Do your attitudes dispose you to want to process different kinds of information?

- **Emotional State** Do the intensity, quality and value (positive, neutral or negative) of your feelings facilitate your memory?

- **Motivation** Are your goals consistent with what you need to learn and remember?

4. Potential

- **Expertise** Do your knowledge and skills enable you to perform memory tasks better than most of the population?

- **Memory Competence** How able are you to perform the memory tasks confronting you at a certain time?

- **Personal Style** Will your normal approach (relaxed/tense; careless/careful) to memory tasks facilitate the task you are attempting?

Improving Your Readiness **for Memory Tasks**

Once you have evaluated the readiness of the various memory modes, there is a variety of things you can do to remedy any deficiencies, optimize your modes for memory tasks and avoid memory failure. If you cannot manage to put yourself in the best state of memory readiness, see if you can avoid a situation where your memory will be tested. Alternatively, if you know your memory modes are in good shape, go ahead with confidence. There are a number of steps you can take to improve each memory mode.

1. **Information** *Control*

Mental Procedures

These work by guiding the thought processes that foster memory. The procedures that best help people avoid memory failure are often specific to the kind of situation that causes a failure. These procedures have been discussed, situation by situation, earlier in this book.

Physical Environment

Avoid wasting your energy on memory tasks when you can use external aids. (For example, several companies sell electronic cheque-books that will carry out the arithmetic and balance your account; reminder devices are invaluable if they sound alarms whenever medicine is to be taken; files, drawers and cupboards, etc. enable us to find something we want without the effort of remembering exactly where we put it.) A written reminder leads to remembering more often than just a mental note. An object placed by the doorway will work better than a written reminder or a note. Your spouse, significant other, friend or boss in the doorway will remind you even better.

Social Environment

If your memory fails when you are with friends, you can always tell them that you are not on top form that day. Otherwise, they may feel that you think they are not worth the effort.

Confidence If you do not know the people you are with, you should try to remain confident about your memory. Do not overstate or understate what you remember; doing so may damage your credibility.

Conversational Skills These can help you remember to say what you want to say and also to register what others have said. For example, if you cannot recall information that others are asking you for, try repeating what you and others have just said. Repetition helps you notice what others have said, delays the input of new information and gives your memory time to work, making it more likely that you will remember. Another skill involves buying time for retrieval of hard-to-remember information by asking questions or referring questions to another person.

2. *Strength*

Physical State

Eat a well-balanced diet. Avoid eating too much before important memory tasks. Get enough sleep. Schedule memory tasks for the peak times during the day when you are strongest and most attentive. Stay in shape.

Health

Treat major and minor illnesses promptly. If you are ill, it is advisable to avoid mental tasks, including memory tasks, whenever possible. Almost all illnesses cause some discomfort and discomfort makes it harder to pay attention. If you have an event coming up that involves mental activity (giving a speech, taking an exam, presenting a lecture, going for an interview) and you are sick, postpone it if you can. If you cannot get out of it, get a lot of rest, over-prepare and avoid doing any work immediately before the event.

Chemical State

If you really want to avoid memory failure, maintain a healthy chemical state. Avoid substances such as coffee, tea, fizzy drinks and other stimulants that can make you jumpy. Make sure you are not using substances or medicines that could make you jittery or dull and sleepy. Most antihistamines and cold medicines have this effect and so do most tranquillizers, some antidepressants and, of course, sleeping pills. If you are taking medication, check the information that came with the medication to see whether it might interfere with memory performance. Look in a reference book or call your doctor or pharmacist if you suspect that a medicine has side-effects which hinder memory, even if the information enclosed does not mention this possibility.

Control alcohol, the 'amnesia food'. Alcohol, marijuana and other mind-altering drugs impair memory performance immediately after use and possibly indefinitely. If relaxation is the issue, there are safer ways to relax than by taking mind-altering drugs.

3. *Inclination*

Attitude

The only way to register material that you dislike is to pay a lot more attention than you usually do. Change negative attitudes into positive ones if you can. It is wrong to think that people can do something just by believing that they can. If some of your memory abilities are good, you want to know this. Likewise, if some of your memory abilities are poor, you want to know this too. Instead of a positive attitude, develop a set of realistic attitudes toward what tasks your memory is or is not good at. Once you have done this, you can make the best use of your memory.

Emotional State

Do not let life's problems pile up on you. If your emotions are too intense, calm your feelings by rest and relaxation. If this is not enough, share your emotional problems with someone you trust. If you are in a cheerful, positive frame of mind, you will learn and remember more easily than when you are feeling pessimistic or depressed.

A poor emotional state reduces your power to focus attention. Efforts to change a bad emotional state will improve your memory. Manage your stress so that it does not get too low or too high. If you feel confused, find a spot where you can rest and avoid others. On the other hand, avoid boredom or you may overlook cues which you need to respond to.

Relax when you can. Exercise, both aerobic and yoga, is beneficial to memory performance. It may sound silly but lying on a bed and hanging your head down over the edge can sometimes help you to commit to memory information that you have recently heard or read.

Motivation

Efforts to improve a bad motivational state will also improve your memory performance. If a negative motivational state can be changed into a positive one, it is highly likely that your memory performance will be excellent. If you are feeling nothing positive about a task, try to figure out what positive consequences will occur when you perform it correctly.

4. *Potential*

Expertise

Everyone is better at doing some things than others. Make a list of the things that you are best at. Study and practise what you are already good at in order to make yourself better still. Being good at a task means that you know a lot about that task, you remember information about that task especially well and you learn such information more easily than other information. Knowing your strengths allows you to avoid memory failure and to enjoy the success that happens when your memory performs well.

Memory Competence

Everyone is better at some memory tasks than others. Some people are better at learning than they are at remembering. Knowing what kinds of memory tasks you find difficult is very useful in avoiding memory failure and remaining successful at memory tasks. Practise the memory tasks that you are already good at in order to make yourself better still. If you are poor at a particular memory task, such as recalling something you have previously learned, practise at that task will make you better.

Personal Style

Decide what your own approach to memory tasks is: are you careful or careless? Evaluate where you direct your awareness: is it on your thoughts or on what is going on around you? Knowing your style gives you more control over success and failure at memory tasks. If you realize that someone, say your boss, expects you to behave differently from your normal style, you can make an extra effort to behave in the way that enables you to avoid memory failure.

* * *

To avoid memory failures you must take account of your biological and social nature. In a nutshell, you can avoid many memory failures if you pay attention to the environment and your social context, and if you are in a good physical, emotional, and mental state when you attempt the memory task.

CHAPTER FIVE

The Lessons of **Memory Failures**

It should be quite clear from reading this book that, as far as memory failures are concerned, the news is both good and bad.

The bad news is that sometimes little or nothing can be done to avoid particular memory failures, because it is the situation that puts you in a position where memory failure cannot easily be avoided. This is particularly true where:

- You are distracted by other matters which are important, such as a baby crying.

- Cues or prompts on which you have become used to relying, perhaps from your partner, fail for no obvious reason.

- Cues or prompts vanish, such as the rain stopping when your have put your umbrella to one side.

- Major life events preoccupy your mental life, such as bereavement – or winning the lottery!

- You are put in an unusual and highly stressful situation, such as travelling by air.

- Your memory, which has been reliable before without any memory aids, fails due to a cluster of unusual circumstances.

As we have seen, there are strategies which can help to reduce memory failures in these situations, and being aware of these situations is in itself helpful. However, it is not really useful to blame yourself, or other people, when memory failure does strike in these situations.

The good news is that there are both general strategies and strategies for specific situations which can help to reduce the likelihood of memory failure in future.

Strategies for **Reducing Memory Failures**

1. Check What *You Need to Remember*

In general terms, a major cause of memory failures is neglecting to check what you need to do or what you have done. Time and again what emerges is a failure to check: where you have parked; what you have packed; the time of departure; whether you have left anything in your hotel room; whether you have your house keys; that you have taken away your takeaways; that you have remembered your partner's birthday, your Christmas card list, etc. Sloppy monitoring of what you need to remember is present in many kinds of memory failure.

2. Be Aware of *Distracting Influences*

Certain kinds of situation are particularly prone to induce memory failure, particularly if you are distracted from normal on-going activities. As noted above, there is sometimes little that can be done about this, but being aware that distraction from an on-going activity can affect memory should make you more sensitive to the danger. For example, if you know that you are more likely to forget to pay for goods if you are highly distracted by a major row with your partner, you can cue yourself to be more aware that you must pay for goods in this situation. If you are distracted by your children just as you are leaving your car, make doubly sure that you have taken the car keys with you.

3. Use *Memory Prompts*

Try to arrange, as far as possible, for the world to help your memory by setting up memory prompts. These could include a special table by the door for takeaways; a special diary for birthdays and anniversaries; a bleeping electronic car key to find your car; checklists for ensuring that you have all the requirements for travel; notes when you have to give talks or go to a meeting, etc. If something is important, it can never be wrong to arrange reminders so that you end up remembering what you want to do.

4. Plan *Ahead*

Take an interest in what you will need to remember at a future time and, where necessary, use memory strategies to ensure that you will remember facts for exams, names and faces, points to make at meetings and speeches, etc. If you do not pay attention to what is going on, you will not remember it later! Despite the claims of some educationalists that using memory aids is a low-level activity, you should always use them if you find them helpful. Remember, it is you, not them, who will pass or fail your exams.

5. Keep Everything *in its Place*

Never put things in unusual places for safety. Whenever possible, keep things on your person or put them in a particular place reserved for them, e.g. a particular hook in your house for your key, a particular drawer for your passport. Also place things in their appropriate place as soon as you can or you might well find you have forgotten to put your passport back in its drawer and cannot remember where you last had it.

6. Keep *Fit*

Try to stay 'memory fit'. Both physical and emotional health have major effects on memory. They affect how well you take in what is going on around you and how well you manage to remember what you have stored in your memory. Tiredness and emotional upsets are bad for memory. Physical fitness allows you to pay much more attention to what is going on.

7. Be *Courteous*

Observe memory courtesy. If you see someone who needs a helping hand, help them, but not too obviously. If someone cannot remember your name, give them information which will enable him/her to put you in context – but *never* make people feel that their memory is inadequate. Phone your dinner guests to check that everything is all right, and to confirm the time – do not assume they have forgotten! Do not be too hard on people who have let you down.

***

Of course, a book of this kind cannot give you all the answers to the problem of memory failures. What we hope to have shown you is that many of the failures which people experience and worry about are common to nearly everyone, and that it usually pays to be philosophical about them, but that there are things you can do to stop them happening if you wish. However, while it is important to prevent important memory failures by taking action beforehand, it is unrealistic to spend too much time trying to prevent *all* the trivial memory failures that may happen in the future. Sometimes you will make mistakes by not remembering – but that's life!

Epilogue

As we have seen in the course of the book, memory failures can have all sorts of sad consequences. They can also have a lighter side.

Things Lost and Found by Someone Else

The world can indeed be an awful place but kindness shines through from time to time. One type of kind person is the 'memory saviour' – a kind person who saves the day for someone whose memory fails and who is about to face the consequences of this failure. For example, everyone misplaces things but some people misplace more things than others. Fortunately, sometimes when we 'lose' things, a memory saviour picks up what we have lost and returns it to us or, if they cannot figure out who is the owner, hangs the object, or a note describing it, on a Lost and Found bulletin board. Here are a couple of examples of memory saviours whom we have encountered in our lives.

Wizard® Again

I went to a superb conference on computing software. I put my Sharp Wizard® palmtop computer down somewhere but I was not sure where. It could have been on a park bench or in a phone booth. In any event, as soon as I realized my precious Wizard® was missing, I went to the Lost and Found board of the conference. Fortunately, some good Samaritan had picked up my Wizard® and handed it in. Thank you kind person!

D.H.

Briefcase Again

I was flying back from San Francisco. My flight was postponed again and again because of San Francisco fog. The aircraft I was catching was a puddle-jumper and would not offer lunch. Because of the postponements of the departure time, it seemed to me that I would not be getting any lunch for a couple of hours if I did not act fast.

I mentioned this to two of my colleagues and we went to the airport restaurant, which you might think would be prepared for emergencies, but, in fact, was also in postponement mode. We ordered sandwiches. We waited and waited for our food. The flight was announced and we could see from the window that nearly everybody had boarded. One of my colleagues rushed out to tell that airline staff that we were waiting for our lunch. They responded that we had better hurry and it was at about this point that the food arrived. The waitress offered to put the food in a bag. I charged all three meals to my credit account because we did not have time for the waitress to give change to each of us. I signed the slip and, as I was leaving, another waitress – carrying meals for a nearby table – pointed out that somebody had left a bag under the table that we had just vacated. Bless this waitress! I am certain that I would not have realized that I had left my bag until later that day, by which time I would have been in a different airport.

D.H.

The next two anecdotes show how some memory failures bug people for years!

Misplaced Winter Jacket

In 1997 M.G. visited D.H and they went to several places and ate out a lot. D.H.'s naval jacket disappeared at this time. If anyone finds it, D.H. will gladly pay for its return (unless that person is M.G., whom he suspects may have absconded with it).

Misplaced Spectacles

In 1995 D.H.'s family moved to Terre Haute in Washington DC. They had been in their new house for a couple of days and everything was a mess. D.H. got up to take some boxes from the living room to the garage. That was the last time that he saw his gold-rimmed spectacles. He still believes that these spectacles are somewhere in the house, although he searched everywhere. It seems unlikely that anyone would have stolen them, despite their attractive appearance, because his eyes – which already suffer from astigmatism – are going downhill pretty fast. If he were to suspect anyone of taking them, the person would have to be over fifty years old.

Finally we would like to end with an example which shows that the world has 'got it in' for memory experts. They really don't like us!

My Magic Diary®

I forgot that I had left my Magic Diary® (my electronic reminding device) in the pocket of my trousers, which I had left spread out on the floor of my closet. (Since being in the forces, I was in the habit of laying out my trousers in this way so that I could put them on quickly the next day). After I had gone to bed, I decided that I needed an extra nightshirt to keep me warm. I keep my nightshirts on the shelf in my closet above where I laid my trousers. I went into the closet but did not turn on the light. As I reached up for a nightshirt I could hear glass cracking beneath my feet. I turned on the light and realized that I had just crushed my reminding device.

D.H.

Memory failures are a part of life, just like many other unfortunate occurrences, such a tripping and falling down, getting a cold, or having an investment go sour. Unfortunate events cannot be totally eliminated from any sector of life but living well can be arranged. This includes memory. So we wish that:

The highway of life will not give you
Too many turns or bumps
And may you be able to remember where there's a bend or
A hole in the road
So that you will enjoy life's ride as much as possible.

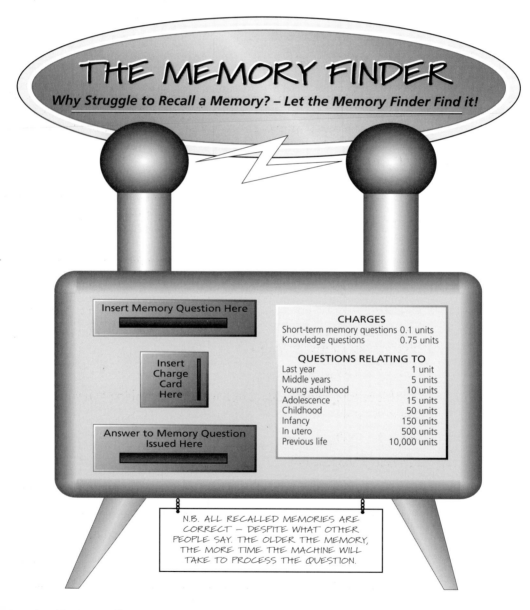

Memory Failure Questionnaire

Now that you have read all these examples of memory failure, you should be very familiar with the variety of ways in which such failures come about. In addition, by this point in the book, you should know a lot about the ways to avoid memory failure. Nevertheless, there are sure to be some occasions when your memory fails in a way which is upsetting or embarrassing, or which has an outcome that makes you really want to avoid it happening in future.

Interviewing **Yourself**

You now know enough to be able to interview yourself about any memory failure. Once you have completed the questionnaire, you will be able to work out how to minimize the chances of this failure happening again.

Memory Failure *Interview*

1. Write a brief account of the memory failure and then answer the questions below:

   ....

   ....

   ....

   Did this failure involve failing to remember a prior event or information learned previously?

   YES ☐   NO ☐

   Did this failure involve failing to remember something you were supposed to do?

   YES ☐   NO ☐

2. Describe where the failure occurred.

   ....

   ....

   ....

   ....

3. What time of day did it occur?

    ....

4. Describe what you were doing at the time of the failure?

    ....

    ....

    ....

5. If others were present, list who they were.

    ....

    ....

    ....

6. Describe how you felt physically before and during the occasion of
    the memory failure.

    ....

    ....

    ....

    ....

    Fatigue   ☐

    Illness   ☐

    Other   ☐

7. Describe how you felt emotionally before and during the occasion of
    the memory failure.

    ....

    ....

    ....

    ....

    Stress   ☐

    Emotionally upset   ☐

    Depressed   ☐

    Unmotivated for the task   ☐

    Detached, too relaxed   ☐

    Other   ☐

8. Were you feeling a great deal of stress?

    YES ☐   NO ☐

9. Were you elated about something?

YES ☐   NO ☐

10. Were there any cues that were removed or disappeared? Did the failure come about because of a change in context?

YES ☐   NO ☐

11. Were you forced to do two things at once?

YES ☐   NO ☐

12. Were you preoccupied with something other than what you were doing?

YES ☐   NO ☐

13. Were you worried?

YES ☐   NO ☐

14. Were you feeling guilty about something?

YES ☐   NO ☐

15. Were you doing something that you really did not want to do? If so, what was it?

YES ☐   NO ☐

16. Did you have to do something that was contrary to a well-established habit?

YES ☐   NO ☐

17. Did you expect that someone else would do whatever it was you had to remember?

YES ☐   NO ☐

18. Did you fail to do what you were supposed to because you were interrupted?

YES ☐   NO ☐

19. Did you fail to do what you were supposed to do because you were interrupted by another task with a higher priority?

YES ☐   NO ☐

20. Did you fail to remind yourself of what was to be done?

YES ☐   NO ☐

21. Did you fail to notice a cue that would normally remind you?

YES ☐   NO ☐

22. Had you become used to cues?

YES ☐   NO ☐

23. Was there an unexpectedly long interval between agreeing to do something and when you had to do it?

YES ☐   NO ☐

24. Was the interval filled with distracting activity?

YES ☐   NO ☐

25. Did you fail to monitor the steps of the task carefully enough?

YES ☐   NO ☐

26. Did the task have to be completed in stages and did you lose track of the stages?

YES ☐   NO ☐

27. Describe your impression of any other factors that you believe could have been responsible for the failure?

....

....

....

....

28. Did you fail to complete the task because of a distraction at the time of the memory task?

YES ☐   NO ☐

29. Did you fail at the task because you did not use external aids when you could have?

YES ☐   NO ☐

30. Did you fail at the task because you relied on others to help you remember and they failed to do so?

YES ☐   NO ☐

31. Did you fail at the task because you didn't get the correct details about the task in the first place?

YES ☐   NO ☐

32. Did you fail at the task because you underestimated its difficulty?

YES ☐   NO ☐

33. Did you fail at the task because there was not enough opportunity to rehearse what you had to remember or to practise the desired response?

YES ☐   NO ☐

Evaluating *Your Answers*

You should now read all your answers to the questionnaire. When you have done so, decide what you think the cause(s) of your memory failure was/were. Then list them below in order of importance.

If you feel that there was just one cause of your memory failure, list only one cause. If you feel that more than one cause was involved, list the additional causes.

In our experience, most memory failures can be attributed to three or four causes, although, in some cases, there may be additional causes. However, the fifth or later causes usually add little to the explanation of the memory failure. Also, in developing a plan to avoid a certain kind of memory failure, it is usually too distracting to try to control more than three or four factors. Thus, we recommend listing only three or four causes although, of course, you are free to list however many you want.

When evaluating your answers, indicate how many causes you feel were responsible for your memory failure and what they were.

1. Simple memory failure (one causal factor):

    ....

    ....

    ....

2. Complex memory failure (two or more simultaneous causal factors – in order of importance):

    (a) ....

    ....

    (b) ....

    ....

    (c) ....

    ....

    (d) ....

    ....

    (e) ....

    ....

You have now completed the memory-failure interview about one of your memory failures. No doubt you have identified some, or all, of the principle reasons for your memory failing. You may feel that your memory was not up to the task in hand. You may also feel that the failure was made more likely because you did not make use of your physical environment or your social context (e.g. friends), or because of your inadequate physical state, emotional state or memory potential. Or you may feel that life conspired against you in a diabolical manner, i.e. it was a case of sheer bad luck!

Clearly, different failures are due to different combinations of factors. Nevertheless, the elements of your memory failure are to be found in the preceding evaluation. Total prevention of memory failures seems impossible but reducing their frequency is definitely feasible and we wish you the greatest success in eliminating them. If you do achieve 100 per cent success, please get in touch with us – we will want to visit and seek your advice on how to do likewise!

Further **Reading**

Herrmann, D., Yoder, C. and Gruneberg, M. (2000) *Memory and its Practical Uses*. New York: Allyn and Bacon.

Gruneberg, M. and Herrmann, D. (1998) *Your Memory for Life*. London: Blandford Press/New York: Sterling Publishing.

Herrmann, D. (1995) *Supermemory*. London: Blandford Press/New York: Sterling Publishing.

Herrmann, D., Raybeck, D. and Gutman, D. (1993) *Improving Student Memory*. Seattle: Hogrefe and Huber.

Gruneberg, M. (1987–98) *Linkword French, German, Spanish, Italian*. Lincolnwood II: NTC/Bristol: Interaktive. www.linkword.co.uk

Searleman, A. and Herrmann, D. (1994) *Memory from a Broader Perspective*. New York: McGraw Hill.

Gruneberg, M. and Morris, P. (1992) *Aspects of Memory*: *The Practical Aspects*. London: Routledge.

Reason, J. and Mycielska, K. (1982) *Absent Minded? The Psychology of Everyday Lapses and Everyday Errors*. Engelwood Cliffs, New Jersey: Prentice Hall.

Herrmann, D. (1982) 'Know thy memory: the use of questionnaires to assess and study memory.' *Psychological Bulletin*, 92: 434–52.

Index